GOODMAN'S FIVE-STAR STORIES

More
CH!LLS

12 More Chilling Tales and Exciting Adventures

With Exercises to Help You LEARN

P9-DEY-051

More Chills

12 More Chilling Tales and Exciting Adventures

WITH EXERCISES TO HELP YOU LEARN

by Burton Goodman

JAMESTOWN PUBLISHERS

a division of NTC/Contemporary Publishing Group
Lincolnwood, Illinois USA

TITLES IN THE SERIES

Adventures	Level B	After Shocks	Level E
More Adventures	Level B	Sudden Twists	Level F
Chills	Level C	More Twists	Level F
More Chills	Level C	Encounters	Level G
Surprises	Level D	More Encounters	Level G
More Surprises	Level D	Conflicts	Level H
Shocks	Level E	More Conflicts	Level H

More Chills

Editorial Director: Cynthia Krejcsi
Executive Editor: Marilyn Cunningham
Project Editor: Christine Lund Orciuch
Production: Thomas D. Scharf
Cover design: Kristy Sheldon
Cover illustration: Bob Eggleton

ISBN: 0-89061-859-3

Published by Jamestown Publishers,
a division of NTC/Contemporary Publishing Group, Inc.,
4255 West Touhy Avenue,
Lincolnwood (Chicago), Illinois 60712-1975 U.S.A.
© 1997 by Burton Goodman
All rights reserved. No part of this book may be reproduced,
stored in a retrieval system, or transmitted in any form or by any means,
electronic, mechanical, photocopying, recording, or otherwise,
without prior permission of the publisher.
Manufactured in the United States of America.

7 8 9 10 11 12 13 14 15   116 / 055   10 09 08 07 06 05 04 03

Contents

To the Student

There are 12 very exciting short stories in *More Chills*. I have picked these stories because I like them so much. I believe that you will like them too.

These stories will give you hours of reading fun. And you will enjoy doing the exercises that follow each story.

The exercises will help you LEARN important reading and literature skills:

LOOKING FOR FACTS IN THE STORY

EXAMINING VOCABULARY WORDS

ADDING WORDS TO A PARAGRAPH

READING BETWEEN THE LINES

NOTING STORY ELEMENTS

LOOKING FOR FACTS IN THE STORY helps you find key facts in a story. Sometimes these facts are called *details*.

EXAMINING VOCABULARY WORDS helps you strengthen your vocabulary skills. Often, you can figure out the meaning of a new word by looking at the words around the unfamiliar word. When you do this, you are using *context clues*. In each story, the vocabulary words are printed in **boldface type.** If you wish, look back at these words when you answer the vocabulary questions.

ADDING WORDS TO A PARAGRAPH helps you strengthen your reading *and* your vocabulary skills. This part uses fill-in, or cloze, exercises.

1

READING BETWEEN THE LINES helps you sharpen your *critical thinking* skills. First, you will have to think about what happened in the story. Then you will have to figure out the answers.

NOTING STORY ELEMENTS helps you understand some important elements of literature. Some story elements are *plot, character, setting,* and *mood.* On page 5 you will find the meaning of these and other words. If you wish, look back at those meanings when you answer the questions.

Another part, **THINKING MORE ABOUT THE STORY,** gives you a chance to think, talk, and write about the story.

Here is the way to do the exercises:

- There are four questions for each of the LEARN exercises above.

- Do all the exercises.

- Check your answers with your teacher.

- Use the scoring chart at the end of each exercise to figure out your score for that exercise. Give yourself 5 points for each correct answer. (Since there are four questions, you can get up to 20 points for each exercise.)

- Use the LEARN scoring chart at the end of the exercises to figure your total score. If you get all the questions right, your score will be 100.

- Keep track of how well you do by writing in your Score Total on the **Progress Chart** on page 136. Then write your score on the **Progress Graph** on page 137. By looking at the Progress Graph, you can see how much you improve.

I know that you will enjoy reading the stories in this book. And the exercises that follow the stories will help you LEARN some very important skills.

Now . . . get ready for *More Chills!*

Burton Goodman

The Short Story—Important Literary Words

Characterization: how a writer shows what a character is like. The way a character acts, speaks, thinks, and looks *characterizes* that person.

Main Character: the person the story is mostly about.

Mood: the feeling that the writer brings about, or creates. For example, the *mood* of a story might be happy or sad.

Plot: the action or events that take place in a story. The first thing that happens in a story is the first action or event that takes place in the *plot*.

Setting: where and when the story takes place. The *setting* is the time and the place of the action in a story.

Theme: the main idea of the story.

1

Playmate

by Leslie A. Croutch

I was in the kitchen when Bobby came rushing through the door. "Hey, Mom," he called. "Can Ricky come over for supper tonight?"

Betty paused. "Who's Ricky, dear?" she asked.

Bobby said, "He's the new boy who moved in next door."

"Is he a nice boy?"

Bobby made a face. "Sure he's a nice boy," he said.

"What is he like, son?" I asked.

"Oh, I don't know. He's—well, he's different."

We let it go at that. I wanted to ask some questions. But Betty caught my eye and shook her head. My wife is usually right about things like this. So I just smiled and didn't say a word.

It was comfortable on the porch. There was a warm breeze blowing. I was sitting there, half asleep. Betty was reading a book. Suddenly a loud shout broke the **silence** of the summer afternoon.

"Hey! Where is the oilcan?"

Bobby came running around the side of the house. He was in a hurry. Kids are that way. He ran up the steps. Then he shouted again, "Where is the oilcan?"

"I think it's on the shelf in the basement," I said. "Just squeeze the can and the oil will **squirt** out."

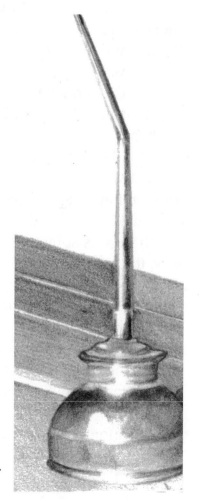

"That's the kind I want," Bobby said. He dashed off.

Betty called out, "What do you need the oil for, Bobby?"

Bobby yelled as he disappeared into the house. "It's for Ricky. He *squeaks*!"

I didn't know what Bobby meant by that. Neither did Betty. But children talk in a funny way sometimes. I closed my eyes, and Betty read her book.

At supper, the food smelled very good. Betty is a wonderful cook.

"Where is Bobby?" she asked as we sat down at the table.

"Oh, he's around somewhere. He's down in the basement, I think."

Just then we heard his footsteps coming up the stairs. Then we heard those of his new friend as Ricky **clattered** up the steps. Bobby went into the kitchen to wash.

"Get another towel for your friend," Betty called.

"Don't need it," Bobby said. "Only need one. Ricky doesn't wash."

I looked at Betty, and she looked at me. Then Betty went into the kitchen.

"Oh, dear," I heard her say a few seconds later.

Betty came back. She held on to the side of a chair. There was a funny look on her face. She didn't look frightened. But she did seem **shocked.** She was shaking her head. Then Bobby and his friend, Ricky, came in.

There was something unusual about the boy. He walked in a stiff kind of way. It looked as though his knees could not bend. There was something strange about his face too. It seemed a little—*shiny.* And there was something funny about his mouth. Of course it opened and closed. But it did that very, very slowly.

I watched the new boy as we ate. He didn't drink his milk the way Bobby did. He held the glass up over his mouth. Then he poured it all down. The *whole* glass of milk quickly disappeared.

He didn't chew his food either, as far as I could tell. He just put the food into his mouth. And down it went! He kept eating that way—like some kind of *machine*—until his plate was empty.

When the meal was over, Bobby was in a hurry to leave. His new friend

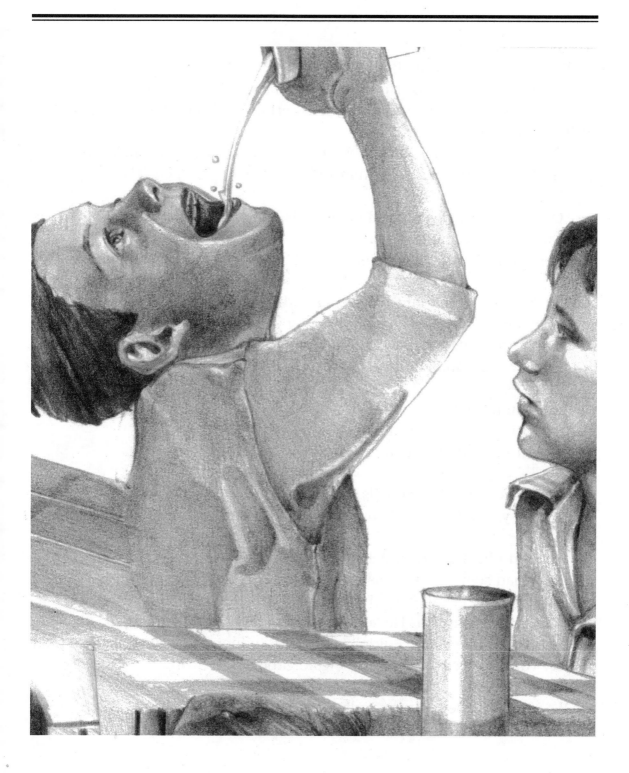

seemed just as eager to go.

When they were gone, Betty stared at me.

She said, "Al, that boy! He's . . . he's—*different*!"

"I know what you mean," I said. "He certainly is! Did you see how he walks? Did you see him eat?"

"But that isn't all. I went into the kitchen to ask him to wash. What do you think I saw? He was oiling himself!"

"He was—*what?*"

"Oiling himself! He squirted oil into his hands. Then he rubbed oil on his neck and his knees and wrists."

"Come on!" I said. "We better get to the bottom of this. Let's find Bobby!"

The boys were building something in the backyard. We could see that they had some long pieces of wood. They were nailing them together.

Bobby was banging away with a hammer.

"How are you doing, Ricky?" asked Bobby.

"Fine," Ricky said.

"Are you using the hammer?"

"No," Ricky answered. "It's faster this way."

"Doesn't it hurt your hand?" asked Bobby.

"No."

"I wish I could drive in nails with my hand."

"It's easy," said Ricky. "You just make a fist and give the nails a good *whack*!"

We didn't hear the rest. We just stood there and stared.

Ricky had some nails in his mouth. He would take one out and hold it against the wood. Then *bang*! He brought his fist down and knocked it in. He didn't use a hammer! He kept banging in the nails just using his fist!

Betty felt a little weak. I didn't feel so well either. We walked back to our house. Then we went to see our new neighbors.

We rang their bell. A very ordinary couple came to the door.

"We're Mr. and Mrs. Hansen," I said. "We live next door."

"Please come in," said the woman. "We thought that you might come by."

"Our name is Robeson," said the man. "I guess that you've met our son."

"Yes," Betty answered. "He came over for supper."

"Oh," said Mrs. Robeson. "So now you know! We've had to move so often. People just don't understand."

"I'm so sorry," Betty said. "But really, he seems like such a nice boy. He is so quiet and polite. But he's—he's—"

"Yes. I know what you mean," Mr. Robeson said. "He *is* different. He's almost seven years old now. But he has been that way ever since he was born."

"Have you taken him to a doctor?" I said very softly.

"A doctor?" Mr. Robeson laughed. "We took him to the best. They found out nothing. They wanted to experiment on Ricky. But we couldn't let them do that. After all, he *is* our son!"

"He grows every year," Mrs. Robeson said. "But no one seems to understand how. Still, nothing ever hurts him. He never gets sick. And there isn't anything that he can't eat."

"Of course, there's the oil," Mr. Robeson said. "He has to oil himself a lot. Or else he gets so stiff he can hardly move."

"What did the doctors say about that?" Betty asked.

"Oh, they used a lot of long words. But they really didn't know."

I said, "Don't you have any idea what might be wrong with him?"

"Wrong?" Mr. Robeson stared at me. "There is *nothing* wrong with him! He has never been ill. He never even gets a cold. He doesn't feel any pain. He is strong, very strong. Why, I've seen him drive in nails with his fist! And he's smart. He's very, very smart. So *you* tell me what's wrong with him!"

He suddenly looked sad. "But we've had to move a lot. People just don't understand. You can't imagine how hard it has been."

We stood at the door. "Don't worry about it," I said. "We won't say a word. We have a son too. Our boy seems to like your boy. That's good enough for us."

That evening Betty and I went up to say good night to Bobby. He was lying on his bed. He was looking out the window. He was staring at the moon.

Bobby turned as we came into the room.

"What are you thinking about, son?" I asked.

"I was just thinking about Ricky, Dad."

"What about Ricky?" asked Betty.

Bobby looked at us. His face was sad. "I was thinking how lucky Ricky is. He can't ever get hurt or be sick. He told me he'll live for hundreds and hundreds of years. And he knows millions of things that I don't know. Oh, he's awfully lucky and awfully smart. I wish that I could be like him."

"What is he like?" Betty asked.

Bobby said, "He asked me not to say. But I guess that it's all right to tell you."

Bobby sighed. "Ricky hasn't got insides the way we do. He's got wires and metal and all kinds of things. He doesn't really have to eat. But he does because he likes the way things taste."

Betty's hand closed tightly over mine. Was Bobby making this up? Was this some kind of game?

"Are there others like Ricky?" I heard Betty ask.

"Oh, yes. Ricky says there are *lots* more. He says he knows ten right here in this city."

"How did he meet them?" I asked.

"Ricky doesn't have to meet them," Bobby said. "He just *thinks*. Then one of them thinks back. And they know."

Bobby lay down and looked at the moon. "I wish I were like Ricky," he said. "Then I could do all kinds of wonderful things. Ricky says when he gets big, his people will rule the world. There won't be any more wars. They won't let people be bad or kill each other. Oh, why can't *I* be like him?"

Bobby's eyes closed. We waited a minute. Then we quietly went out of the room.

"What do you

think?" Betty asked.

"I don't know," I answered. "I really don't know."

Betty said, "I'd like to think it's just a game he's playing."

Since then I've been feeling a little afraid. You are always afraid of things you don't understand. You are always afraid of things you can't stop.

You see, the neighbor's boy still plays with Bobby. The other day I saw them building something near the garage. Bobby was pounding in the nails. But he was using his fist!

LOOKING FOR FACTS IN THE STORY.

How well can you find facts in a story? Put an *x* in the box next to the right answer.

1. At the beginning of the story, Bobby was looking for
   - ❑ a. a toy.
   - ❑ b. an oilcan.
   - ❑ c. his bicycle.

2. Bobby's father thought Ricky's face looked
   - ❑ a. sad.
   - ❑ b. happy.
   - ❑ c. shiny.

3. Mr. Robeson said that Ricky was
   - ❑ a. strong.
   - ❑ b. weak.
   - ❑ c. sick.

4. Bobby wished that he were
   - ❑ a. much older.
   - ❑ b. a little taller.
   - ❑ c. like Ricky.

EXAMINING VOCABULARY WORDS.

Here are four vocabulary questions. Put an *x* in the box next to the right answer. The vocabulary words are printed in **boldface** in the story. You may look back at the words before you answer the questions.

1. A loud shout broke the silence. The word *silence* means
   - ❑ a. darkness.
   - ❑ b. noise.
   - ❑ c. quiet.

2. Ricky's footsteps clattered up the stairs. The word *clattered* means
   - ❑ a. fell down.
   - ❑ b. looked for.
   - ❑ c. made a noise.

3. If you squeeze the can, you will squirt out the oil. The word *squirt* means
   - ❑ a. fill up.
   - ❑ b. force out.
   - ❑ c. pay for.

4. She didn't look frightened, but she did look shocked. The word *shocked* means
   - ❑ a. surprised.
   - ❑ b. delighted.
   - ❑ c. hungry.

	x **5** =	
NUMBER CORRECT		YOUR SCORE

	x **5** =	
NUMBER CORRECT		YOUR SCORE

ADDING WORDS TO A PARAGRAPH.
Complete the paragraph below. Fill in each blank with one of the words in the box. Each word appears in the story. There are five words and four blanks, so one word in the box will not be used.

Can you _____
1

what life would be like without

machines? How would we

manage if all the automobiles,

telephones, and TV sets suddenly

_____ ? Life
2

would _____
3

be very different, indeed. It

would be like living more than a

hundred _____ ago.
4

| disappeared | usually | imagine |
| years | certainly | |

_____ x **5** = _____

NUMBER
CORRECT

YOUR
SCORE

READING BETWEEN THE LINES.
These questions will help you think critically. You will have to think about what happened in the story, and then figure out the answers. Put an *x* in the box next to the right answer.

1. We may infer (figure out) that Ricky was
   - ❑ a. like most children his age.
   - ❑ b. not very smart.
   - ❑ c. some kind of machine.

2. The Robesons expected their neighbors to drop by to
   - ❑ a. have dinner.
   - ❑ b. talk about Ricky.
   - ❑ c. watch TV.

3. The last sentence of the story suggests that Bobby
   - ❑ a. was afraid of Ricky.
   - ❑ b. didn't like to build things.
   - ❑ c. was becoming like Ricky.

4. At the end of the story, Bobby's father was
   - ❑ a. frightened.
   - ❑ b. amused.
   - ❑ c. pleased.

_____ x **5** = _____

NUMBER
CORRECT

YOUR
SCORE

N OTING STORY ELEMENTS.

Some story elements are **plot, character, setting,** and **mood**. Put an *x* in the box next to the right answer.

1. What happened last in the *plot*?
   - ☐ a. Betty told Bobby to get a towel for his friend.
   - ☐ b. Bobby's father saw Bobby pounding in nails with his fist.
   - ☐ c. Bobby's parents visited their neighbors.

2. Which sentence *characterizes* Ricky?
   - ☐ a. He did well in school.
   - ☐ b. He never caught a cold.
   - ☐ c. He was very different.

3. Where is the story *set*?
   - ☐ a. in and around the homes of two neighbors
   - ☐ b. in a playground
   - ☐ c. in a place far from Earth

4. The *mood* of the story is
   - ☐ a. very funny.
   - ☐ b. very sad.
   - ☐ c. scary and strange.

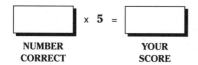

	× **5** =	
NUMBER CORRECT		**YOUR SCORE**

THINKING MORE ABOUT THE STORY. Your teacher might want you to write your answers.

◆ Mr. Robeson said that there was "nothing wrong" with his son. What did he mean by that? Why did the Robesons have to move so often?

◆ Why do you think Bobby and Ricky became such good friends?

◆ "Playmate" is the kind of story known as science fiction. What things in the story make it science fiction?

Use the boxes below to total your scores for the exercises. Then write your score on pages 136 and 137.

☐	**L** OOKING FOR FACTS IN THE STORY
+	
☐	**E** XAMINING VOCABULARY WORDS
+	
☐	**A** DDING WORDS TO A PARAGRAPH
+	
☐	**R** EADING BETWEEN THE LINES
+	
☐	**N** OTING STORY ELEMENTS
▼	
☐	**SCORE TOTAL:** Story 1

How Now Purple Cow

by Bill Pronzini

Floyd Anselmo was driving across his ranch one day in September. That's when he saw the purple cow. There it was on the top of a hill. It was eating some grass.

Floyd stopped his truck at the side of the road. He pulled up the brake. Then he leaned across the seat. He closed his eyes and opened them again. But the cow was still there. A *purple* cow.

"I must be seeing things," Floyd said to himself. "I'm seeing things."

Floyd stared at the cow. "Disappear!" he whispered softly to himself. But the cow didn't go away.

Floyd shook his head and got out of the truck. He stood at the side of the road and looked up at the hill. The cow was still there.

"The next thing you know, I'll be seeing pink elephants," Floyd told himself.

He walked around in front of the truck. He jumped over the white fence and climbed slowly up the hill. When he was halfway up, Floyd took another look. The purple cow was still there. It stood out against the green grass and the brown and white of the other cows.

Floyd moved closer to where the cow was **grazing.** Floyd circled around the cow. The cow paid no attention to him.

"Listen here," Floyd said to the cow. "You can't be real."

The cow kept on chewing, **ignoring** him.

"Cows aren't purple," Floyd told the cow.

The animal shook its tail and went on eating.

Floyd looked at the cow for a very long time. Then Floyd sighed and walked down the hill.

His wife was in the kitchen when Floyd came back a little later.

"You're back early," she said.

"Amy," said Floyd. "There's a purple cow on a hill down the road."

Amy looked at Floyd and kept drying the dishes. "I just made some fresh coffee, dear," she said.

Floyd pulled at his ear. "I said there's a purple cow on a hill down the road."

"Of course," said his wife, as she put away the dishes.

Floyd went outside. He saw Hank Raines, one of his workers, coming back from the barn.

"Good morning, Mr. Anselmo," said Hank.

"Good morning," said Floyd. Then he said slowly, "Hank, I saw this purple cow on a hill down the road."

Hank looked at him.

"At first, I thought I was probably seeing things. But I went right up to it. And it was purple, all right. I can't figure it out."

"Well," Hank said, looking strangely at Floyd.

"You haven't seen it by any chance, have you, Hank?"

"Me? No, sir," said Hank.

Floyd nodded. "Want to come out with me and have a look at it?"

Hank paused. "Well," he said, "there are a few things I've got to take care of right now."

"Maybe later," said Floyd.

"Sure," Hank told him, moving quickly away. "Maybe later."

Floyd went back into the house. He picked up the telephone on the table. He called Jim Powell, the editor of the newspaper in town.

"This is Floyd Anselmo," he said when Powell answered the phone.

"What can I do for you, Floyd?"

"Well," Floyd said slowly. "I was driving through my ranch a while ago. I saw this purple cow eating some grass on top of a hill."

There was silence on the other end.

"Jim? Are you there?" Floyd asked.

"A purple cow?" Powell finally said.

"That's right," Floyd told him. "A purple cow."

There was another silence, shorter this time. Then Powell laughed. "You're putting me on, joking with me, right?"

"No. I'm serious," said Floyd.

"Look, Floyd, I'm a busy man," Powell said. "With all these silly calls about flying saucers I've been getting lately, I haven't had time to finish my work." Suddenly Powell began to chuckle. "Say, Floyd, maybe this purple cow of yours came in on one of those flying saucers people claim they've been seeing."

"Jim," Floyd said slowly. "I don't know anything about flying saucers. All I know is there's a purple cow on a hill on my ranch. If you want to come out here, I'll show it to you."

Powell was quiet for a moment. Then he said, "All right. I'll come out. But if this is some kind of joke . . . "

"The hillside I'm talking about is a mile onto my land just along the highway," Floyd told him. "I'll meet you there."

"I'll see you in thirty minutes," Powell said unhappily. Then he hung up the phone.

Floyd started to leave. His wife came into the room just as he reached the door. "Where are you going, dear?" she asked.

"To meet Jim Powell."

"What for?"

"To show him the purple cow I saw."

Amy looked worried. "Floyd, you've been working too hard lately," she said. "Floyd . . ."

"I'll be back in an hour or so," Floyd answered. Then he stepped outside.

He started his truck and drove down the road. When he reached the hillside, he saw that the purple cow had moved farther down the hill. It was now only a few feet away from the white fence.

Floyd stopped the truck and got out. He walked to the fence. He climbed over it, and stood facing the cow.

The cow continued to eat the grass. It did not seem to know that Floyd was there.

Floyd walked slowly up to the cow. Very carefully, Floyd put out his hand and touched the cow's head. Then Floyd stepped back.

"I was beginning to have some doubts," said Floyd. "But you're real. And you're certainly purple. That's for sure."

The cow **shifted** its legs.

"Where did you come from anyway?" asked Floyd. "Jim Powell said something about flying saucers. Now, I don't believe in those things. But—"

Floyd suddenly stopped talking. His eyes were staring at

his hand—the hand he had touched the animal's head with seconds earlier.

His fingers were turning purple. His arm was turning purple too.

For a second, Floyd had an urge to turn and run. It quickly passed.

After a moment, the animal raised its head. For the first time, it looked at Floyd.

In a questioning **tone,** the cow said, "Moo?"

"Moo," answered Floyd.

There were two purple cows on the hill when Jim Powell arrived a few minutes later.

LOOKING FOR FACTS IN THE STORY. How well can you find facts in a story? Put an *x* in the box next to the right answer.

1. Floyd saw a purple cow while he was
   - ❑ a. walking back from the barn.
   - ❑ b. driving across his ranch.
   - ❑ c. looking out of the kitchen window.

2. Floyd's wife thought that Floyd
   - ❑ a. had been working too hard.
   - ❑ b. wasn't working hard enough.
   - ❑ c. was joking with her.

3. Jim Powell said he would meet Floyd in
   - ❑ a. ten minutes.
   - ❑ b. thirty minutes.
   - ❑ c. an hour.

4. When Floyd touched the cow, his fingers began
   - ❑ a. to hurt.
   - ❑ b. to shake.
   - ❑ c. to turn purple.

EXAMINING VOCABULARY WORDS. Here are four vocabulary questions. Put an *x* in the box next to the right answer. The vocabulary words are printed in **boldface** in the story. You may look back at the words before you answer the questions.

1. The cow was grazing on top of the hill. The word *grazing* means
   - ❑ a. eating grass.
   - ❑ b. falling down.
   - ❑ c. sleeping.

2. When Floyd spoke to the cow, it kept on chewing, ignoring him. The word *ignoring* means
   - ❑ a. attacking.
   - ❑ b. smiling.
   - ❑ c. not listening to.

3. The cow shifted its legs. The word *shifted* means
   - ❑ a. moved.
   - ❑ b. hurt.
   - ❑ c. looked at.

4. In a questioning tone, the cow said, "Moo?" The word *tone* means
   - ❑ a. worry.
   - ❑ b. sound.
   - ❑ c. time.

	x **5** =	
NUMBER CORRECT		**YOUR SCORE**

	x **5** =	
NUMBER CORRECT		**YOUR SCORE**

25

A

DDING WORDS TO A PARAGRAPH.
Complete the paragraph below.
Fill in each blank with one of the
words in the box. Each word
appears in the story. There are five
words and four blanks, so one word
in the box will not be used.

You have _____

1

never watched the way a cow eats

grass. A cow does not have sharp

teeth in the _____

2

of its mouth. So the cow tears out

the _____ by

3

moving its head from side to side.

Then it always _____

4

the grass twice.

highway	front	chews
probably		grass

R

EADING BETWEEN THE LINES.
These questions will help you
think critically. You will have to
think about what happened in the
story, and then figure out the
answers. Put an *x* in the box next
to the right answer.

1. We may infer (figure out) that
   Floyd
   - ❑ a. met Jim Powell.
   - ❑ b. turned into a purple cow.
   - ❑ c. saw pink elephants.

2. Which sentence is true?
   - ❑ a. Hank Raines thought that
     Floyd was acting strangely.
   - ❑ b. Hank also saw the purple
     cow.
   - ❑ c. Floyd's wife was not
     worried about Floyd.

3. The purple cow probably came
   from
   - ❑ a. Floyd's barn.
   - ❑ b. the back of Floyd's truck.
   - ❑ c. a flying saucer.

4. At the end of the story, Jim
   Powell probably felt
   - ❑ a. happy.
   - ❑ b. amazed.
   - ❑ c. tired.

[ ] x **5** = [ ]

NUMBER
CORRECT

YOUR
SCORE

[ ] x **5** = [ ]

NUMBER
CORRECT

YOUR
SCORE

NOTING STORY ELEMENTS.

Some story elements are **plot, character, setting,** and **mood**. Put an *x* in the box next to the right answer.

1. What happened last in the *plot*?
   - ❑ a. Floyd told his wife he saw a purple cow.
   - ❑ b. Two purple cows were on the hill.
   - ❑ c. Floyd called Jim Powell.

2. Who is the *main character* in the story?
   - ❑ a. Floyd Anselmo
   - ❑ b. Hank Raines
   - ❑ c. Jim Powell

3. The story is *set*
   - ❑ a. in a newspaper office.
   - ❑ b. on a highway one summer.
   - ❑ c. on a ranch in September.

4. The *mood* of the story is
   - ❑ a. scary and strange.
   - ❑ b. very funny.
   - ❑ c. very sad.

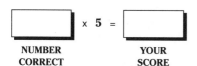

NUMBER CORRECT x **5** = **YOUR SCORE**

THINKING MORE ABOUT THE STORY.

Your teacher might want you to write your answers.

- ◆ Why did Floyd touch the purple cow? Why did he touch it carefully?
- ◆ Jim Powell said he had gotten many calls about flying saucers. Explain why this is important in the story.
- ◆ At the end of the story, the cow asked "Moo?" and Floyd answered "Moo." What do you think they said to each other?

Use the boxes below to total your scores for the exercises. Then write your score on pages 136 and 137.

L **OOKING FOR FACTS IN THE STORY**

+

E **XAMINING VOCABULARY WORDS**

+

A **DDING WORDS TO A PARAGRAPH**

+

R **EADING BETWEEN THE LINES**

+

N **OTING STORY ELEMENTS**

▼

SCORE TOTAL: Story 2

Trapped

by Carmen Hansen

Dorcas sleepily opened her eyes. She looked slowly around her room. The morning sunlight came shining in.

The first thing she saw was the little copper teapot. It stood on the shelf next to some books. How bright it looked **gleaming** in the sunshine. Dorcas thought, "How much brighter it would look if I polished it."

Dorcas swung her legs over the bed. She went into the bathroom. She washed. Then she dressed. Today was the second day of school. And what could be nicer than being awakened by sunlight?

Her parents were eating breakfast when Dorcas came into the kitchen. She was carrying the teapot with her.

"Good morning, honey," said her father. His voice was deep and strong. He was always so cheerful in the morning. He ate his breakfast and smiled at everyone. Her mother was different.

"Come on, Dorcas," she said. "Hurry up and eat. You'll be late for school. I was just about to come in and wake you up. What are you doing?"

Dorcas bent down to get the copper cleaner. It was in a drawer next to the sink. "I'm just going to take a minute," she told her mother. "I want to shine this teapot. It's getting so dull."

"Really! You can always think of something to do the first thing in the morning. Why don't you wait? You can do that later."

Dorcas sighed. She put down the little teapot. She woke up filled with joy. And suddenly that joy had slipped away. She sat down at the table. There wasn't any use in **arguing** with her mother. Dorcas had learned that long ago. Dorcas just did what her mother said. Sometimes Dorcas felt trapped.

Her father held out his coffee cup. Dorcas watched her mother pour the black stuff into his cup. The steam floated up. It mixed with the sunshine. The morning wasn't as pretty as it had been a little while ago.

Her father said, "Dorcas. I have a surprise for you."

Dorcas looked at her mother. "I wonder what it is."

Her mother pushed down the handle on the toaster. "Oh, I don't know," she said. "We'll soon see."

Dorcas was pouring some juice when her father came back. He was **grinning** happily. His two gold teeth almost seemed to glow. On his hand sat a huge grasshopper. It was the biggest grasshopper that Dorcas had ever seen. Her father held the thing right under her nose.

"See. I found him outside this morning. I thought you could take him to your biology class."

Dorcas looked at the big green thing. It **crouched** on her father's open hand. It looked very frightened. Then one of its thin legs suddenly moved. Dorcas's head moved back.

"Daddy, please. I don't want him jumping into my food."

Her father took a step back. "Oh, he won't jump now," he said. "He's cold. I thought that you could put him in a jar. I thought you could take him to school for the other kids to see. You will be studying grasshoppers, you know."

Dorcas tried to smile. "All right, Daddy. And thank you very much. What shall we do with him now?"

"I'll get a jar. Where's a jar?" He was already on his way out of the room, looking for a jar.

Dorcas rode to school with her father. She watched the grasshopper. It jumped wildly inside the glass jar. There were some pieces of grass in the jar. Her father had put them there for the grasshopper to eat. The grass stuck to the grasshopper's legs. A few pieces stuck out from behind its head.

Dorcas felt tears come to her eyes. She turned her face so that her father wouldn't see. She didn't even know if her teacher wanted them to bring in things like this. After all, it was only the second day of school.

Dorcas sighed. Her father was always trying to be so helpful. Sometimes he was a little *too* helpful. In some ways he was like a small boy.

But she loved him. And she wouldn't have hurt his feelings for anything. She smiled as she got out of the car.

"See you later, Daddy. Thanks for the ride."

"Good-bye, honey. And good luck with the grasshopper. You know, the teacher might really be able to use him."

The car roared off. Dorcas hurried into the school. She balanced the jar on top of her books. It was lucky that biology was her first class. She wouldn't have to look at the jar much longer. She wouldn't have to look at the frightened thing inside it.

The bell rang. Dorcas walked slowly to her biology class. Some of the kids in the hall were staring at the jar. What could she do? Then a thought flashed into her mind. Of course! She would just let the grasshopper go!

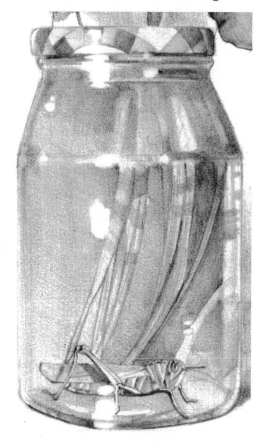

She pictured herself walking out to the yard. She pictured herself taking the top off the jar. She pictured the grasshopper leaping out of its jail. She pictured it hopping away in joy. But those pictures were just in her mind. The poor grasshopper remained in the jar. There was nothing it could do to get free.

Dorcas reached the door of the biology class. She looked down at the grasshopper. It was quiet in its glass cage.

"I'm sorry," she said to it softly.

She wanted to set it free. But

she couldn't let it go, of course. There would be questions at home. Daddy would feel hurt. Her mother would scold her and make her stay in her room.

Dorcas heard the late bell ringing. She took a deep breath. Then she walked into the class. No, she couldn't let the grasshopper go. There was nothing she could do. Nothing at all. At that moment, Dorcas felt trapped. She felt nearly as trapped as the poor grasshopper.

LOOKING FOR FACTS IN THE STORY.
How well can you find facts in a story? Put an *x* in the box next to the right answer.

1. The first thing that Dorcas saw in the morning was
   - ❑ a. a book on a shelf.
   - ❑ b. a little copper teapot.
   - ❑ c. her father eating breakfast.

2. Dorcas's mother was afraid that Dorcas would
   - ❑ a. refuse to eat breakfast.
   - ❑ b. be late for school.
   - ❑ c. set the grasshopper free.

3. How did Dorcas get to school?
   - ❑ a. She walked there.
   - ❑ b. She took a bus.
   - ❑ c. She rode there with her father.

4. At the end of the story, Dorcas
   - ❑ a. took the grasshopper into the class.
   - ❑ b. went into the yard.
   - ❑ c. let the grasshopper go.

EXAMINING VOCABULARY WORDS.
Here are four vocabulary questions. Put an *x* in the box next to the right answer. The vocabulary words are printed in **boldface** in the story. You may look back at the words before you answer the questions.

1. The teapot was gleaming in the light. The word *gleaming* means
   - ❑ a. falling.
   - ❑ b. shining.
   - ❑ c. whistling.

2. There was no point arguing with her. The word *arguing* means
   - ❑ a. hiding from.
   - ❑ b. offering a gift to.
   - ❑ c. giving reasons to prove you are right.

3. Her father was grinning happily. The word *grinning* means
   - ❑ a. smiling.
   - ❑ b. working.
   - ❑ c. eating.

4. The grasshopper crouched on her father's hand. The word *crouched* means
   - ❑ a. leaped high in the air.
   - ❑ b. bent, ready to jump.
   - ❑ c. ran very quickly.

	x 5 =	
NUMBER CORRECT		**YOUR SCORE**

	x 5 =	
NUMBER CORRECT		**YOUR SCORE**

ADDING WORDS TO A PARAGRAPH.

Complete the paragraph below. Fill in each blank with one of the words in the box. Each word appears in the story. There are five words and four blanks, so one word in the box will not be used.

Most _____
1

are only one to three inches

long. Although grasshopppers

are _____
2

small, they can jump surprisingly

long distances. The grasshopper's

back legs are longer and stronger

than its front _____ .
3

Its back legs give the grasshopper

the power to _____
4

very far.

quite	grasshoppers	studying
	leap	legs

☐ × **5** = ☐

NUMBER
CORRECT

YOUR
SCORE

READING BETWEEN THE LINES.

These questions will help you think critically. You will have to think about what happened in the story, and then figure out the answers. Put an *x* in the box next to the right answer.

1. We may infer (figure out) that Dorcas
   ☐ a. got to school late.
   ☐ b. didn't get along very well with her mother.
   ☐ c. didn't like her father.

2. Dorcas didn't let the grasshopper go because she
   ☐ a. was afraid of it.
   ☐ b. didn't like it.
   ☐ c. didn't want to have problems later at home.

3. Dorcas and the grasshopper were alike because they both
   ☐ a. felt trapped.
   ☐ b. lived in the same house.
   ☐ c. didn't like to get up early.

4. How did Dorcas feel at the end of the story?
   ☐ a. happy
   ☐ b. excited
   ☐ c. helpless

☐ × **5** = ☐

NUMBER
CORRECT

YOUR
SCORE

N OTING STORY ELEMENTS.

Some story elements are **plot, character, setting,** and **mood.** Put an *x* in the box next to the right answer.

1. What happened last in the *plot*?
   - ❑ a. Kids in the hall stared at the jar.
   - ❑ b. Dorcas's father gave her a grasshopper.
   - ❑ c. Dorcas went to get the copper cleaner.

2. Who is the *main character* in the story?
   - ❑ a. Dorcas
   - ❑ b. Dorcas's mother
   - ❑ c. Dorcas's father

3. The story is *set*
   - ❑ a. on the first day of school.
   - ❑ b. on the second day of school.
   - ❑ c. during the third week of school.

4. What is the *mood* of the story?
   - ❑ a. funny
   - ❑ b. very frightening
   - ❑ c. sad

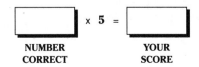

	x 5 =	
NUMBER CORRECT		YOUR SCORE

THINKING MORE ABOUT THE STORY. Your teacher might want you to write your answers.

◆ Should Dorcas have told her father that she didn't want to take the grasshopper to school? Give reasons.

◆ If you were Dorcas, would you have let the grasshopper go? Explain your answer.

◆ Do you think "Trapped" is a good name for the story? Why? Think of another interesting title for the story.

Use the boxes below to total your scores for the exercises. Then write your score on pages 136 and 137.

L OOKING FOR FACTS IN THE STORY

\+

E XAMINING VOCABULARY WORDS

\+

A DDING WORDS TO A PARAGRAPH

\+

R EADING BETWEEN THE LINES

\+

N OTING STORY ELEMENTS

▼

SCORE TOTAL: Story 3

4

A Terrible Night

based on a story by Anton Chekhov

It was a terrible night! It was an awful night! It was one of the worst nights of my life!

It all started at the magic show. My friend, Peter, and I went there together. We heard that the magician was great. His name was Rompkin. And he *was* very good.

Rompkin was tall and thin. He wore a long black coat. He had a deep voice, and his eyes burned like coals. Rompkin did some amazing tricks. He made furniture fly through the air around the room. He turned a piece of rope into a snake. I mean it became a *real* snake! Peter and I were sitting up front. We saw it very well. The snake twisted and turned. It began to hiss. Then Rompkin changed the snake back into the piece of rope.

There was another trick that I liked very much. Rompkin told people things about themselves—things that only they could know. These things turned out to be true. The people were amazed that he knew these things.

At the end of the show, Rompkin said he was able to see into the future. He told what he thought was going to happen. Then he looked at Peter and me. He pointed a finger in our direction. Rompkin yelled, "The end of your life is near!" Then the curtain came down. The show was over!

Well, I was not happy to hear what Rompkin said. It was just a show, of course. But still it was frightening.

We left to go home. Peter went one way. I went the other.

It was a terrible night. It was very cold, and there was no moon. And then, for no reason at all, the streetlights went out. I made my way home through the dark, empty streets. I can tell you, I was scared. I could hear Rompkin's voice ringing in my ears, "The end of your life is near!"

I climbed up the stairs to my apartment. It was on the fourth floor. I opened the door and went in. I turned on a lamp. I heard the wind howling across the roof. The rain beat loudly against my window. And then, in the middle of the room, I saw—a coffin![1]

I cried out and stepped back. I blinked my eyes, and I looked again. In the middle of the room there stood a coffin!

I rushed out. I hurried downstairs as fast as I could. I was lucky I didn't fall down the steps and break my neck. When I got to the street, my heart was pounding. I felt very weak.

I would have been less surprised to discover that my room was on fire. I would have been less surprised to find a thief or a wild dog there. Those things, at least, can be explained. But how could a coffin have suddenly appeared in my room? Where had it come from? And was—was there a dead body inside?

I thought about it all. My door was locked while I was away. Only my best friends knew where I kept the key. But the coffin certainly had not been left by my friends. Could an undertaker[2] have brought that coffin to the wrong address? No! What undertaker would leave a coffin without being paid?

Rompkin had said that the end of my life was near. Was this *my* coffin?

I caught my breath. Then I said to myself, "Ivan. Stop acting like a fool. You didn't really see a coffin in your room. You only *imagined* that it was there. It was just your nerves! That magician, Rompkin, worried you. You thought about his words all the way home. And it's such a terrible, dark, and **gloomy** night!"

Still, I did not feel comfortable going back to my room. I was afraid I might see the coffin again. But I couldn't stay in the street in that storm. So I decided to go to my friend Boris's place. Boris lived in a building that was not far away.

---

1. coffin: a box in which a dead person is buried.
2. undertaker: a person whose business is preparing and burying people who have died.

My friend was not at home. But I knew where he hid the key. I found it at once. Then I unlocked the door and went inside. It was very dark. I put on the light and turned around.

I saw a coffin in the middle of the room!

I cried out. I ran out of the room and back into the street.

"I must be losing my mind!" I told myself. "I'm seeing things! There can't be a coffin in every room I enter."

My head began to **ache,** and my knees were shaking. Rain was pouring down. The wind was as sharp as a knife. And I—I was losing my mind!

What could I do? Where could I go? Then I remembered that Peter lived nearby. I ran, without stopping, straight to his place. As I was climbing up the stairs, I heard a loud cry. A door slammed shut. There were footsteps on the stairs. A moment later, a man in a coat came dashing down the steps.

"Peter!" I exclaimed, recognizing my friend. "Is that you, Peter?"

I grabbed him by the arm. "Tell me what's the matter!"

Peter stopped short. He was pale. His hands were trembling. "Is that you, Ivan?" he asked, in a shaking voice. "Is that really you? You look as though you've seen a ghost."

"But what about *you*?" I said. "You look scared to death!"

Peter said, "It's great to see you—if it really is you. I'm seeing things! My nerves are shot! When I got back to my room just now, I thought that I saw— a coffin!"

I couldn't believe my ears!

Peter's voice was filled with fear. He said, "Rompkin pointed at us—at you or me. He said that the end was near! Then I get back to my room and find a *coffin!*"

I told Peter about the coffins that *I* had seen.

For a moment, we gazed at each other. Then Peter said, "So now what do we do?"

We stood on the staircase for a very long time. Finally, Peter said, "I do not wish to go back upstairs. But if you are willing to return to your room, I will go with you."

Again we went out into the wind and the rain. When we got to my apartment, I slowly pushed open the door. There stood the coffin.

Peter said, "We must find out whether or not this coffin is—empty."

I did not move. Peter looked at me. Then he bent over and removed the **lid.** We both looked inside.

There was no dead body. But we did find a letter. It said:

My dear Ivan:

My father's business has suddenly gotten very bad. He is the best coffin maker in town. But right now he owes more money than he has. If only we had a little more time, he could pay off all his bills. But tomorrow they're coming to take away everything he owns.

Yesterday, we decided to hide everything of **value** that he has. Most of his property, of course, is coffins. I am sending you a coffin, my friend. It will not be necessary for you to hold it for more than a week. I hope that this is not too much to ask. I have sent a coffin to every one of our old, dear friends.

With many thanks,
Serge Nevisky

The coffin maker's business got better, I am happy to say. I understand that he makes and sells many other things too. But the other day I heard that his business is bad again. That makes me very nervous. Now, every evening when I come home from work, I am afraid of what I might find in my room.

LOOKING FOR FACTS IN THE STORY. How well can you find facts in a story? Put an *x* in the box next to the right answer.

1. At the beginning of the story, Ivan and Peter went to
   - ❑ a. the home of a friend.
   - ❑ b. a place to eat.
   - ❑ c. a magic show.

2. How did Ivan get into Boris's apartment?
   - ❑ a. Boris let him in.
   - ❑ b. Ivan found the key.
   - ❑ c. Ivan forced the door open.

3. What did Ivan and Peter find in the coffin?
   - ❑ a. nothing at all
   - ❑ b. a dead body
   - ❑ c. a letter

4. Serge said that his father's business
   - ❑ a. had suddenly gotten very bad.
   - ❑ b. was doing very well.
   - ❑ c. was about the same.

EXAMINING VOCABULARY WORDS. Here are four vocabulary questions. Put an *x* in the box next to the right answer. The vocabulary words are printed in **boldface** in the story. You may look back at the words before you answer the questions.

1. It was a terrible, dark, and gloomy night. The word *gloomy* means
   - ❑ a. joyful.
   - ❑ b. interesting.
   - ❑ c. sad.

2. His head began to ache, and his knees were shaking. The word *ache* means
   - ❑ a. hurt.
   - ❑ b. worry.
   - ❑ c. smile.

3. Peter removed the lid of the coffin. A *lid* is
   - ❑ a. a cover or top.
   - ❑ b. a piece of earth.
   - ❑ c. a note.

4. They hid everything of value. When something has *value,* it
   - ❑ a. is worth nothing.
   - ❑ b. is worth something.
   - ❑ c. is very large.

	x **5** =	
NUMBER CORRECT		**YOUR SCORE**

	x **5** =	
NUMBER CORRECT		**YOUR SCORE**

DDING WORDS TO A PARAGRAPH.
Complete the paragraph below.
Fill in each blank with one of the
words in the box. Each word
appears in the story. There are five
words and four blanks, so one word
in the box will not be used.

I gave my good friend, Pat, a

_____ to my
1
apartment. When it is

_____ for me
2
to be away, Pat waters my plants

and feeds my cat. If I lose my

key, I feel _____
3
knowing that Pat has another. I

am lucky that Pat lives in a

_____ across
4
the street from me.

building	necessary	curtain
comfortable	key	

	x **5** =	
NUMBER CORRECT		**YOUR SCORE**

READING BETWEEN THE LINES.
These questions will help you
think critically. You will have to
think about what happened in the
story, and then figure out the
answers. Put an *x* in the box next
to the right answer.

1. Ivan thought he was losing his
   mind because
   ❑ a. he kept seeing coffins.
   ❑ b. he couldn't sleep.
   ❑ c. nobody believed his story.

2. Which sentence is true?
   ❑ a. Rompkin was short and fat.
   ❑ b. When Peter saw the coffin,
      he acted calmly.
   ❑ c. Serge must have known
      where Ivan hid his key.

3. What did *not* scare Ivan?
   ❑ a. walking in the dark
   ❑ b. learning that Serge's father
      owed money
   ❑ c. hearing that the end of his
      life was near

4. After Ivan and Peter read the
   letter, they probably
   ❑ a. started to cry.
   ❑ b. became more frightened.
   ❑ c. felt better.

	x **5** =	
NUMBER CORRECT		**YOUR SCORE**

NOTING STORY ELEMENTS.

Some story elements are **plot, character, setting,** and **mood**. Put an *x* in the box next to the right answer.

1. What happened first in the *plot*?
   - ❑ a. Peter dashed down the steps.
   - ❑ b. Ivan went to Boris's apartment.
   - ❑ c. Rompkin said, "The end of your life is near!"

2. Who is the *main character* in the story?
   - ❑ a. Rompkin
   - ❑ b. Ivan
   - ❑ c. Peter

3. The story is *set*
   - ❑ a. on a cloudy morning.
   - ❑ b. on a summer afternoon.
   - ❑ c. on a cold, rainy night.

4. The *mood* of the story is
   - ❑ a. scary.
   - ❑ b. very funny.
   - ❑ c. very sad.

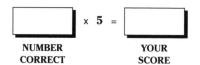

	× 5 =	
NUMBER CORRECT		**YOUR SCORE**

THINKING MORE ABOUT THE STORY. Your teacher might want you to write your answers.

- ◆ Suppose Ivan had not gone to the magic show. Would he have been as frightened when he saw the coffin? Explain.
- ◆ If Ivan had not met Peter on the staircase, how do you think the story would have ended?
- ◆ The letter explains why Ivan received the coffin. Think of another reason to explain how the coffin might have arrived at Ivan's apartment.

Use the boxes below to total your scores for the exercises. Then write your score on pages 136 and 137.

	L OOKING FOR FACTS IN THE STORY
+	
	E XAMINING VOCABULARY WORDS
+	
	A DDING WORDS TO A PARAGRAPH
+	
	R EADING BETWEEN THE LINES
+	
	N OTING STORY ELEMENTS
▼	
	SCORE TOTAL: Story 4

5

The Jade Goddess

by Lin Yutang

Meilan was a young, happy girl. She lived in a large house that had gardens all around it. Her father was Judge Chang. He was the most important judge in the city of Kaifeng in China, where they lived long ago.

One day a distant cousin arrived at the house. His name was Ling Po. He was a tall, handsome fellow, sixteen years old. He was looking for work.

Meilan's mother liked the young man at once. She gave him a job. He worked as a servant, caring for visitors.

Ling Po was a year older than Meilan. They often talked and laughed together. Ling was very bright and full of fun. He told wonderful stories. Meilan enjoyed hearing them.

But Ling was not a good servant. He forgot things. And he made mistakes. So Meilan's mother asked him to work as a gardener. Ling Po loved the flowers and the trees. He was very happy doing that work.

Ling had taught himself to paint. When he had the time, he painted very beautiful pictures. He could also make animals out of clay. They looked so real, you would have thought they were alive.

Everyone in the family liked Ling Po—everyone but Judge Chang. Of course, Meilan liked Ling *very* much. But since they were cousins, marriage seemed out of the question.

When Ling was eighteen, he suddenly announced, "I have found a new job. I am going to be a helper in a shop where they work with jade."

Jade is a very hard stone. It is used to make jewelry. It is not easy to carve jewelry out of jade. Good jewelry made of jade costs a lot of money.

So Ling went to work at his new job. But he continued to live at the house. And he spent even more time with Meilan than he had before.

One day Meilan's mother said to her, "You and Ling are both grown up now. Although Ling is your cousin, you should not see each other so much."

These words made Meilan think. She had never realized that she was in love with Ling Po.

That night she met Ling in the garden. She said, "Mother says that I must not see you so much."

Ling paused, then said, "We are grown up now."

"What does that mean?" Meilan asked.

"It means I love you," Ling Po answered.

"But," said Meilan, "you know that I cannot marry you. And before long, my parents will make me marry some other man."

Ling said, "All that I know is this. Everything you are is wonderful to me. I am happy when you are near. When you are away, I am lonely and sad."

Meilan sighed and asked, "Are you happy now?"

"Yes, Meilan," he answered. "We belong to each other."

Meilan was **confused.** She said, "But you know that we cannot marry."

"Do not say that," answered Ling.

"You must understand," said Meilan.

"I understand only this," said Ling. He took Meilan into his arms. "We were meant for each other. I will not let you go."

Meilan broke away from him and ran to her room.

From that night on she was completely changed. The more she tried to stop their love, the more it grew. They were in love's power.

Meanwhile, Ling Po was learning how to carve jade. He seemed born to carve jade. He *loved* carving jade. He did wonderful work. The owner of the shop was pleased. Rich people came to the shop and bought many pieces there.

One day Meilan's father decided to give his wife a present. He bought a large piece of very beautiful jade. He went to the shop where Ling Po worked.

He said to Ling, "Here is a piece of very fine jade. I would like you to

carve a statue out of this jade. If you do it well, you will receive a rich reward."

Ling looked at the lovely stone. He said, "I will carve a statue out of this jade. I will make a statue of the Goddess of Mercy. It will be the most beautiful statue that anyone has ever seen."

Ling worked for many months. When the statue was finished, it was a wonderful work of art. It was **marvelous** to see. The Goddess's face was like that of the woman he loved.

Judge Chang was delighted. "The face is like Meilan's," he said.

"Yes," Ling answered, proudly. "That is the way I meant it to be."

The Judge gave Ling a great deal of money. And from that day on, everyone knew about Ling. Yet what he wanted most, he could not have. Success meant nothing to him without Meilan.

One day Meilan's parents decided that Meilan must marry the son of a friend. Meilan and Ling were still very much in love. They did not know what to do. Finally they decided to run away.

They went at night through a gate in the garden. But an old servant happened to see them leave. He tried to stop them. He grabbed Meilan and refused to let her go. Ling had no choice. He pushed the servant aside, and the old man fell. He hit his head against a rock and did not move. Meilan and Ling looked down at the dead man on the ground. Then, filled with fear, they began to run.

The next day the family discovered that Ling and Meilan were gone. The servant was found lying dead in the garden. Judge Chang flew into a **rage.** "I shall cover the earth!" he cried. "I will find Ling Po and punish him!"

Meilan and Ling went to the city of Kian in the south of China. There they were married.

"There is good jade here," said Ling. "This is where I will work."

Meilan was worried. "Do you think that you should carve jade again?" she asked. "People will recognize your work."

"But that was what we planned to do," he said.

"That was before the servant died," she answered. "They think we killed him. Can't you do some other kind of work? Why don't you make animals out of clay?"

"Why?" said Ling. "I do very fine work with jade."

"That is the trouble," said Meilan.

"I don't think we have to worry," answered Ling. "Kian is a thousand miles away from Kaifeng. Nobody here knows us."

Meilan had taken some of her jewelry before they left. They sold the jewelry and bought good jade for Ling to carve. Ling opened a shop. He made very beautiful things. Before long, many people came to the shop to buy his work.

"Dear, I am worried," Meilan said to Ling. "You are getting to be very well known. I am afraid that they will find out who we are."

"There is no need to worry," said Ling.

One day a man walked into the shop. He looked around. Then he said, "Are you not Ling Po? Didn't you once live in Kaifeng? Did you not run away with the daughter of Judge Chang?"

Ling Po said, "I do not know Judge Chang. I have never been to Kaifeng."

Meilan watched this from the back of the shop. When the man left, Meilan came out. She told Ling, "That man works in my father's office."

The next day the man came in again. The man said, "I believe that you are Ling Po."

"Who is this Ling Po?" asked Ling.

"I will tell you," said the man. "He is wanted for killing a servant. He ran away with Judge Chang's daughter. He has also stolen her jewelry. If you are not Ling Po, show me your wife. I will be satisfied when I see she is not Judge Chang's daughter."

"I am running a shop here," said Ling. "I must ask you to leave."

The man smiled at Ling. "I shall be back with the police," he said.

As soon as the man left, Meilan and Ling packed their things. They hired a boat and sailed far up the river. Finally they stopped at the city of Hanshoy.

There Ling sold the jade pieces that he had brought.

"Listen to me now," said Meilan. "This time we must open a shop and sell things made of clay. You can sell the clay animals that you make. Later things may change. Then you can carve jade again."

Ling set up a shop and made animals out of clay. But in his heart he wanted to carve jade.

One day he picked up a clay animal he had just made. He **crushed** the clay between his fingers. "Mud!" he exclaimed. "Why should I work with mud when I can work with jade!"

So, without telling Meilan, he made two beautiful pieces out of jade. One afternoon he sold them to a stranger, who offered a very high price.

A week later, three police officers came to Ling's shop. They had orders to arrest Ling Po and Meilan and to bring them back to Kaifeng. The man from Judge Chang's office was with the police.

"We will go with you," Ling told the officers. "Just let us pack a few things."

Ling Po and his wife were allowed to go to the back of the shop, while the officers waited in front.

It was a very sad moment for them both. Meilan burst into tears. Ling Po kissed his wife and said good-bye. He knew that he would never see her again. Then he jumped down from the window.

"I will love you always," Meilan called softly.

"And I will love you forever," Ling Po answered.

Ling took one last look at Meilan as she stood at the window. She raised her arm and waved good-bye to him forever.

After Ling had disappeared in the distance, Meilan calmly entered the front of the shop. Very slowly she began putting things into a bag. After a while, the officers became suspicious. They searched the shop. But Ling Po had gone.

When she returned home, Meilan discovered that her mother had died.

Her father was glad, in a way, that Ling had escaped. For he would not have known what to do with him. Still, he could not forgive the man who had brought shame to his family.

Years passed and no news about Ling ever came. Meilan never saw his face again. But every day she looked at the beautiful Goddess of Mercy that Ling had made. And for as long as Meilan lived, Ling remained alive in her heart.

OOKING FOR FACTS IN THE STORY.
How well can you find facts in
a story? Put an *x* in the box next to
the right answer.

1. Meilan's mother asked Ling Po to
   work
   - ❑ a. as a gardener.
   - ❑ b. in Judge Chang's office.
   - ❑ c. in a shop where jade was
     sold.

2. Why did Ling Po push the
   servant?
   - ❑ a. The servant pushed Ling
     first.
   - ❑ b. The servant hit Ling with
     a rock.
   - ❑ c. The servant refused to let
     go of Meilan.

3. Meilan didn't want Ling to carve
   jade because she was afraid that
   - ❑ a. people would recognize
     Ling's work.
   - ❑ b. they would not make
     enough money.
   - ❑ c. they would run out of jade.

4. Ling got away from the police by
   - ❑ a. hiding under the bed.
   - ❑ b. jumping out of the window.
   - ❑ c. climbing onto the roof.

	x 5 =	
NUMBER CORRECT		**YOUR SCORE**

EXAMINING VOCABULARY WORDS.
Here are four vocabulary questions. Put an *x* in the box next to the
right answer. The vocabulary words
are printed in **boldface** in the story.
You may look back at the words
before you answer the questions.

1. Meilan was confused and did not
   know what to do. The word
   confused means
   - ❑ a. mixed up.
   - ❑ b. able to understand.
   - ❑ c. very sorry.

2. The statue was marvelous to see.
   The word *marvelous* means
   - ❑ a. difficult.
   - ❑ b. easy.
   - ❑ c. wonderful.

3. When his daughter ran away,
   Judge Chang flew into a rage.
   The word *rage* means
   - ❑ a. terrible anger.
   - ❑ b. much thought.
   - ❑ c. loud crying.

4. Ling crushed the clay in his
   hand. The word *crushed* means
   - ❑ a. held up to the light.
   - ❑ b. broke into pieces.
   - ❑ c. washed very carefully.

	x 5 =	
NUMBER CORRECT		**YOUR SCORE**

DDING WORDS TO A PARAGRAPH.
Complete the paragraph below.
Fill in each blank with one of the
words in the box. Each word
appears in the story. There are five
words and four blanks, so one word
in the box will not be used.

Jade is a hard stone that is often

used for making _____.
                              1
Although most jade is green, the

_____ may be
          2
white or red or many other colors.

Jade has always been very highly

prized in _____. The
                          3
finest pieces in the world were

_____ there more
          4
than 500 years ago.

| reward jewelry China |
| carved stone |

READING BETWEEN THE LINES.
These questions will help you
think critically. You will have to
think about what happened in the
story, and then figure out the
answers. Put an *x* in the box next
to the right answer.

1. Meilan's mother probably
   realized that
   ❑ a. Meilan was falling in love
        with Ling.
   ❑ b. Ling would kill a man.
   ❑ c. Ling would never be rich.

2. The man who worked in Judge
   Chang's office probably
   ❑ a. had never seen Meilan.
   ❑ b. knew nothing about Ling.
   ❑ c. had been searching for
        Ling.

3. Ling was found because he
   ❑ a. told friends who he was.
   ❑ b. used his real name.
   ❑ c. continued to carve jade.

4. Which sentence is true?
   ❑ a. Meilan didn't love Ling.
   ❑ b. Ling's beautiful jade pieces
        led a trail to him.
   ❑ c. Ling stole Meilan's jewelry.

| | x **5** = | |

NUMBER
CORRECT

YOUR
SCORE

| | x **5** = | |

NUMBER
CORRECT

YOUR
SCORE

N OTING STORY ELEMENTS.

Some story elements are **plot, character, setting,** and **mood.** Put an *x* in the box next to the right answer.

1. What happened first in the *plot*?
   - ❑ a. Ling made a statue.
   - ❑ b. Ling married Meilan.
   - ❑ c. Ling bought a shop.

2. Which sentence *characterizes* Ling Po?
   - ❑ a. Everyone liked him.
   - ❑ b. He did not enjoy making animals out of clay.
   - ❑ c. He was a tall, handsome man who seemed born to carve jade.

3. Where is the story *set*?
   - ❑ a. in the United States
   - ❑ b. in China long ago
   - ❑ c. in a store today

4. Which sentence tells the *theme* of the story?
   - ❑ a. A judge becomes angry.
   - ❑ b. A woman warns her husband to do a different kind of work.
   - ❑ c. Carving jade, a man's love, leads to the loss of his wife.

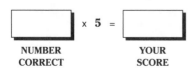

	× 5 =	
NUMBER CORRECT		YOUR SCORE

THINKING MORE ABOUT THE STORY. Your teacher might want you to write your answers.

◆ Should Ling Po and Meilan have gotten married? Give reasons for your answer.

◆ Suppose Ling Po sent a letter to Judge Chang explaining what happened and saying he was sorry. What do you think Judge Chang would have done? How do you think the story would have ended?

◆ Do you think that Ling Po ever carved jade again? Explain.

Use the boxes below to total your scores for the exercises. Then write your score on pages 136 and 137.

☐ +	**L** OOKING FOR FACTS IN THE STORY
☐ +	**E** XAMINING VOCABULARY WORDS
☐ +	**A** DDING WORDS TO A PARAGRAPH
☐ +	**R** EADING BETWEEN THE LINES
☐ ▼	**N** OTING STORY ELEMENTS
☐	**SCORE TOTAL:** Story 5

6

The Mirror

by Judith Bauer Stamper

Hugo Hoogen lived alone. He had no family or friends. He did not even have a pet.

Hugo was a bookkeeper. Monday through Friday he worked in an office. Every day he sat down at his desk. It was in the corner of the office. He added up long lists of numbers. Every two weeks he sent paychecks to the people who worked in the office. He almost never spoke to the people. He just wrote their names on the checks.

Hugo spent the weekends alone. On Saturdays he watched television. And he carefully read every piece of mail that he had received during the week. There was never a letter from anyone he knew. The letters were always from people who wanted to sell him something.

On Sundays Hugo read the newspaper. Then he took a walk.

Hugo really didn't mind living alone. In fact, he liked it. The truth was that Hugo didn't like people. But sometimes Hugo could tell that he had been alone for too long. Sometimes when he *had* to talk to someone, his voice sounded funny to him. It sounded like the voice of a stranger.

When that happened, Hugo went out to eat in a restaurant. He would speak to the person who took his order. He would ask one or two questions. He would listen to what the people at the other tables were saying. That usually got him back to **normal**.

One Monday morning Hugo woke up at exactly 7:30, as he did every morning. It had rained all weekend. Hugo had not left his apartment for two days. He had not been able to take a walk on Sunday. He had stayed inside all day watching television and reading newspapers.

Hugo slowly got out of bed. His head felt very funny this morning. He went into the bathroom and turned on the cold water. He splashed water all over his face. He tried to clear his head. But still he felt strange.

After he had dried his face, Hugo looked in the mirror. He always did that in the morning. Somehow, he didn't seem to be thinking straight this morning. And what he saw in the mirror didn't make sense. He looked at himself in the mirror. He stared straight at his reflection. He looked at his eyes—at his nose and his mouth. He looked at his whole face. But the more he looked at himself, the more it seemed to him that he was looking at the face of a stranger.

"That's not me," he said to himself. "That can't be me!" But when he moved his face up and down, the face in the mirror moved up and down too.

Hugo shut his eyes for a few seconds. He shook his head back and forth. Then he looked in the mirror again. The stranger's face was still there. It hadn't gone away. It was staring at him.

"What's happening here?" wondered Hugo. He put his hands up to his face. It felt the same. Suddenly he had to be certain that he was still himself. He ran to the closet and threw open the door. His clothes were all there. They were hanging neatly in rows, arranged by color. He opened a dresser drawer and reached for his wallet. He took out a credit card. When he saw his name on the card, Hugo sighed with relief.

Then he looked in the mirror at the top of the dresser. The face of the stranger was looking back at him.

"That isn't *me*," Hugo **declared** in a trembling voice. "I don't look like *that*."

Hugo put on one of his oldest suits. It was one that he had worn dozens of times. He felt a little more comfortable wearing that suit. It made him feel more like himself.

Hugo went into the kitchen. He poured himself a bowl of cereal. As he picked up the big cereal spoon, he saw the stranger's face in the spoon. It was staring at him. "I don't look like *that*," Hugo repeated.

Suddenly he thought, "I know how I can prove I don't look like that! There must be a picture of me somewhere." But he couldn't find a picture.

No one had ever taken a picture of him. At least, he couldn't remember anyone ever taking his picture. Hugo began to shake. Wasn't there any way he could prove that he wasn't the stranger in the mirrors?

It was now 8:15. He had to be at his desk in forty-five minutes. Hugo didn't know what to do. He couldn't go into his office looking like a stranger. But he couldn't stay home either. It was the first day of the month. The people in his office had to get their paychecks today.

Hugo got ready to go to the office. He locked the door to his apartment and went outside. His neighbor, Mrs. Reynolds, **approached** him on the street.

"Good morning, Mr. Hoogen," she said.

Hugo nodded at her. Then he **realized** what that meant. He looked like

his old self to Mrs. Reynolds! He almost went back to his apartment to look in a mirror. But then he remembered that there was a mirror at the front of the bus that he took to get to his office.

Hugo walked to the bus stop and waited. He hummed a song. He felt better now. The bus pulled up. Hugo got on. As he gave the driver his money, Hugo bent down to look in the mirror. The stranger stared back with a grin on his face!

Hugo made his way to a seat. He rode all the way to his office with his eyes shut. But now and then, he opened his eyes and looked in the window by his seat. Whenever he did that, he saw the stranger's face there.

At 9:00, Hugo was in his office and was at his desk. He sat there and waited for someone to notice. But no one did. The people who worked there acted the way they always had. They paid no more attention to him than they usually did.

Hugo couldn't understand what was happening. He looked in the mirror several times that day. Each time he saw the stranger's face staring back at him. He looked like a stranger. And no one had even noticed!

After work, Hugo went home and went straight to bed. He closed his eyes. He waited in the darkness until sleep put his worried mind to rest.

When Hugo woke up the next morning, he was afraid to look in the mirror. But he had to shave to go to work. It was hard to shave the stranger's face. Hugo's hands kept shaking.

The same thing happened Wednesday morning and Thursday morning.

On Friday morning, Hugo woke up at 7:15. He lay in bed for a long time. He didn't want to get up. He felt funny having a stranger's face. He stayed in bed for nearly an hour.

But the fear of being alone with the face all day forced him out of bed. He decided he would go to work even though he was late. He went into the bathroom and began to shave. He looked in the mirror. There was his old face! His own face was back in the mirror again!

Hugo felt his face. It was really him! This was the way that he really looked! He let out a wild laugh. The stranger had gone! He had disappeared.

Hugo was himself again!

Hugo finished shaving. He dressed and rushed out of the house. He did not even finish his breakfast. He was eager to go to work now. He was eager to have people see him.

He locked his door. Then he went outside. Mrs. Reynolds passed him in the street. She looked at him in a funny way and didn't say good morning. But Hugo was too happy to notice that she was acting strangely.

He hurried up the steps of the bus and handed the driver some money. Hugo leaned over. He saw his own face smiling back at him in the driver's mirror.

As he rode along, Hugo looked in the window every few minutes. He wanted to be sure that the reflection he saw in the window was really his. It always was.

At 9:30, Hugo pushed open the door to his office. Someone called to him from across the room. But he didn't pay attention. He wanted to get to his desk. He was already late.

Hugo moved quickly across the room to his desk in the corner. He sat down in his chair. He noticed then that the room had become very quiet. As a matter of fact, there was no sound at all.

Hugo smiled as he saw Miss Rose walking toward his desk.

"Yes, Miss Rose," he said.

Miss Rose stopped a few feet from his desk. "Who are you?" she asked.

Hugo laughed at her joke. Miss Rose was being very friendly today.

"Why are you sitting at Mr. Hoogen's desk?" she demanded.

Hugo stopped laughing. He looked into Miss Rose's eyes. The truth slowly crept into Hugo's mind. Miss Rose was looking at a stranger. He could see that she didn't recognize him. She had no idea who he was.

Hugo gripped both sides of his desk very tightly.

"Who are you?" Miss Rose repeated.

But Hugo Hoogen didn't answer. His mind was too busy spinning around and around . . . into total madness.

How well can you find facts in a story? Put an *x* in the box next to the right answer.

1. What did Hugo Hoogen do at work?
   - ❑ a. He read all the mail.
   - ❑ b. He spoke to the other workers.
   - ❑ c. He added up long lists of numbers.

2. When Hugo's voice sounded funny to him, he went
   - ❑ a. to a doctor.
   - ❑ b. to visit some friends.
   - ❑ c. to eat in a restaurant.

3. Hugo had trouble shaving because
   - ❑ a. his hands shook when he shaved the stranger's face.
   - ❑ b. he was tired from being up all night.
   - ❑ c. he was worried about losing his job.

4. At the end of the story, Miss Rose
   - ❑ a. told Hugo a joke.
   - ❑ b. asked Hugo who he was.
   - ❑ c. told Hugo to leave.

	x 5 =	
NUMBER CORRECT		**YOUR SCORE**

E XAMINING VOCABULARY WORDS. Here are four vocabulary questions. Put an *x* in the box next to the right answer. The vocabulary words are printed in **boldface** in the story. You may look back at the words before you answer the questions.

1. Hugo's voice sounded strange. It did not sound normal. The word *normal* means
   - ❑ a. very different.
   - ❑ b. very loud.
   - ❑ c. the same as usual.

2. "That isn't me!" Hugo declared. The word *declared* means
   - ❑ a. asked.
   - ❑ b. wondered about.
   - ❑ c. said strongly.

3. She approached Hugo and said "Good morning." The word *approached* means
   - ❑ a. came near.
   - ❑ b. went away.
   - ❑ c. worried about.

4. He realized that she knew him. The word *realized* means
   - ❑ a. forgot.
   - ❑ b. understood.
   - ❑ c. wanted.

	x 5 =	
NUMBER CORRECT		**YOUR SCORE**

A

DDING WORDS TO A PARAGRAPH.
Complete the paragraph below.
Fill in each blank with one of the
words in the box. Each word
appears in the story. There are five
words and four blanks, so one word
in the box will not be used.

The Sunday _____
1

is almost always the biggest

newspaper of the week. Some

Sunday papers are so thick,

they weigh _____
2

pounds. It takes some people

all week to read their

_____ newspaper.
3

In fact, many readers do not

have time to _____
4

reading all the parts of the paper.

arranged	several	finish
newspaper	Sunday	

	x **5** =	
NUMBER CORRECT		**YOUR SCORE**

R

EADING BETWEEN THE LINES.
These questions will help you
think critically. You will have to
think about what happened in the
story, and then figure out the
answers. Put an *x* in the box next
to the right answer.

1. Which is a sign that something
   unusual was happening to Hugo?
   - ❑ a. He read the newspaper.
   - ❑ b. He took a walk.
   - ❑ c. His voice sounded like the
     voice of a stranger.

2. One day Mrs. Reynolds saw
   Hugo and did not say good
   morning. She probably
   - ❑ a. was angry at him.
   - ❑ b. was too tired to talk.
   - ❑ c. didn't recognize his face.

3. On Friday, Hugo woke up at 7:15
   rather than 7:30 as he always did.
   This suggests that
   - ❑ a. he wasn't tired.
   - ❑ b. he was "not himself."
   - ❑ c. his clock was broken.

4. At the end of the story, Hugo was
   - ❑ a. sorry for Miss Rose.
   - ❑ b. scared and upset.
   - ❑ c. glad he went to work.

	x **5** =	
NUMBER CORRECT		**YOUR SCORE**

NOTING STORY ELEMENTS.
Some story elements are **plot, character, setting**, and **mood**. Put an *x* in the box next to the right answer.

1. What happened last in the *plot*?
   - ❏ a. Hugo got on the bus.
   - ❏ b. Miss Rose didn't recognize Hugo.
   - ❏ c. Hugo looked in the mirror several times at work.

2. Which sentence *characterizes* Hugo?
   - ❏ a. He was very friendly.
   - ❏ b. He lived an exciting life.
   - ❏ c. He lived alone and didn't really like people.

3. The *mood* of the story is
   - ❏ a. funny.
   - ❏ b. frightening.
   - ❏ c. happy.

4. Which sentence tells the *theme* of the story?
   - ❏ a. Strange events in a man's life drive the man mad.
   - ❏ b. Everyone needs friends.
   - ❏ c. You should always get to work on time.

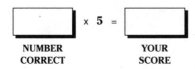

NUMBER CORRECT   x **5** =   YOUR SCORE

THINKING MORE ABOUT THE STORY.
Your teacher might want you to write your answers.

◆ Hugo had no family or friends. He almost never spoke to anyone. Explain why these facts are important in "The Mirror."

◆ Do you think Hugo's face *really* changed—or did he just imagine that happened? Explain.

◆ The writer has said that this story should be read at "the midnight hour." What do you think she meant?

Use the boxes below to total your scores for the exercises. Then write your score on pages 136 and 137.

L OOKING FOR FACTS IN THE STORY
+
E XAMINING VOCABULARY WORDS
+
A DDING WORDS TO A PARAGRAPH
+
R EADING BETWEEN THE LINES
+
N OTING STORY ELEMENTS
▼
SCORE TOTAL: Story 6

7

The Mail Coach Road

by Amelia B. Edwards

The story I am about to tell you is true. It happened to me. I remember it well. Twenty years have gone by since that night. During that time, I have told this story to just one other person.

As I say, this happened twenty years ago. I had been hiking all day. And I had lost my way. It was not a pleasant place to be lost. All around me were hills. Snowflakes were beginning to fall. The day was very cold, and a storm was coming.

As the sky grew darker, I thought about my wife. She was waiting for me at an inn in Melville. We had been married for only two months. When I left in the morning, I promised her that I would return before dinner. Oh, how I wish I had been able to keep that promise!

The snow kept falling. The night grew darker. I was **weary**, for I had been walking all day. But I *had* to find shelter! I remembered stories about travelers who had gotten lost in the snow. They walked on and on until they finally lay down and slept away their lives. Would that happen to me? To die now, when my life lay bright before me! To die with my dear wife waiting!

Suddenly, I saw a **speck** of light in the dark. I ran toward the light. I found myself face-to-face with a short, bearded man. He was carrying a lantern.

"Thank heavens!" I exclaimed.

The man lifted the lantern and looked at my face. "What for?" he asked.

"For you! I was lost in the snow."

"Folks often get lost around here," he growled. "There is nothing they can do."

"Perhaps not. But now that you're here, I'm not lost. How far is it to the town of Melville?"

"About twenty miles."

"And how far is the nearest village?"

"The nearest village is twelve miles away."

"Then where do you live?" I asked.

"Out there," he said, pointing to the hills.

"You're going home, I suppose."

"Maybe I am."

"Then I'm going with you!"

The bearded man shook his head. "No!" he said loudly. "He won't let you in!"

"We'll see about that!" said I. "Who is *he*?"

"The master of the house."

"Lead the way!" I demanded. "Your master will give me a room and supper tonight!"

The man unhappily led the way through the snow.

I saw something large just ahead in the dark.

"Is that the house?" I asked.

"Yes, it's the house." The man reached into his pocket for the key. As soon as the door was opened, I pushed past the man and hurried inside.

I was in a large, dark room. It was so huge it looked like a barn. Against the walls were bookcases filled with books.

"Go in there," said the man. He pointed to a door at the end of the room.

I walked to the door. I knocked on it loudly and went into the room.

A tall, white-haired old man got up from a table, which was covered with papers and books.

"Who are you?" he asked. "How did you get here? What do you want?"

"James Murray is my name. I came by foot. I want food, drink, and sleep."

"This is not an inn!" the old man said angrily. "Jacob, how dare you let in this stranger!"

"I did *not* let him in," grumbled the man. "He followed me home and pushed his way past me."

"What right do you have to force your way into my house?" said the old man.

"The same right by which I would **cling** to your boat if I were drowning. It is the right to save my life!"

"To save your life?"

"Two inches of fresh snow are already on the ground. By morning the snow will be deep enough to cover my body."

He moved to the window and pulled aside the curtain.

"That is true," he finally said. "If you wish, you may stay tonight. Jacob, bring us supper."

We ate in silence. When we finished, the old man turned to me. He said, "I have lived here for twenty-three years. During that time, I have seen very few people. I have not read a newspaper. You are the first stranger who has entered this house in more than four years. Can you tell me a little about what has happened outside? I am interested in science."

I was no student of science. But I told him all I could about the world of that day. It was 1885.

When I had finished, the old man began to talk. He talked on and on. He seemed to know everything about science.

Then he said, "But there are some things that science *cannot* explain. We call these things spirits, strange powers, and ghosts. I studied those things for many years. Then I wrote a book about them."

The old man's eyes suddenly looked fierce. "Other scientists read my book. They called me a fool! They made fun of me! They laughed at my work! That happened twenty-three years ago. Since then I have lived as you see me now. I have forgotten the world, and the world has forgotten me."

The old man got up and walked to the window. "It has stopped snowing," he said.

"Stopped!" I exclaimed. "If only I could find my way back to the town! But I could not walk a distance of twenty miles tonight."

"Walk twenty miles!" said the old man. "What are you thinking of!"

"Of my wife," I answered. "Of my young wife, who does not know I have lost my way. At this moment, her heart must be breaking with fear."

"Where is she now?"

"At Melville."

"Yes, Melville is twenty miles from here. But are you in such a hurry to leave?"

"I am!"

The old man said, "There is a coach that carries the night mail to Melville. The coach takes the road at a crossroads three miles from here. It will pass along that road an hour from now. If Jacob showed you how to get to that road, do you think you could find it?"

"Easily—and gladly!" I answered.

"Jacob!" called the old man. "Show this stranger the way to the old coach road."

The scientist turned to me. "Good night and good luck!" were his final words.

Outside the wind had died down, but the night was dark and cold. There was not a star in the sky overhead. The only sound was the snow beneath our feet. We walked in silence until Jacob said, "Take the road over there. Follow the fence until you come to the crossroads. At the crossroads, stay to your right and keep following the fence. The mail coach will come along soon."

"Then that is the old coach road?" I asked.

"Yes."

I put my hand in my pocket and gave Jacob some money. He smiled. And, for the first time, he seemed a little more friendly.

Jacob said, "You will see a sign when you get to the crossroads. Be very careful when you pass that sign. The fence there is broken. It has never been fixed since the accident."

"What accident?"

"Nine years ago, the coach was delivering the night mail. The coach hit the fence and went over the cliff. It fell seventy-five feet into the valley below."

"Terrible!" I said. "How many lives were lost?"

"Four men, passengers, were killed. The driver was never found."

"The fence near the sign, you said. I will keep that in mind."

"Good night," Jacob said. Then he turned and went back.

I watched the light of his lantern until it disappeared. Then I began to walk along the road. The night air was very cold. And though I walked very fast, I could not keep warm. My feet were like ice. Finally I stopped. I rested against the fence and looked back down the road.

Suddenly I heard the sound of horses. Then I *saw* the horses! They were coming fast. I saw the carriage behind the horses. This must be the night coach!

Could I have walked past the sign without noticing it? There was no time to think about that. The horses and coach were nearly upon me! I shouted! I waved my hat! The driver stopped the coach. But he did not look down or say a word.

I went up to the coach. I opened the door and looked inside. Three travelers were there. I stepped inside and shut the door. Then I sat down in the empty seat.

The coach seemed even colder than the air outside. I looked at the passengers. All three were men, and all were silent. They did not seem to be asleep. But each leaned back in his corner, as though deep in thought.

"It is very cold tonight," I said to the man next to me.

The man did not speak.

"I cannot remember so cold a winter," I said.

I did not see the man's face in the dark. But I saw that his eyes were staring at me.

I **shivered** from head to foot. "May I close this window?" I asked the man to my left.

The man did not answer or move.

I reached over to pull the window down. As I did, the handle broke off in my hand. I looked more closely at the coach. It was falling apart! The floor under my feet was nearly worn away!

I turned to the third passenger and said, "This coach is very old. The usual mail coach, I suppose, is being repaired."

He did not say a word. He moved his head slowly and looked at me. I shall never forget that face! My heart turned cold at the sight of it. I turn cold now when I think of it. His face was not a living face. It was bony and thin—and *dead*! Only his eyes were alive. They glowed at me.

I turned to look at the other two men. Then I saw that all three passengers were not living men! Only their terrible eyes were alive! And those eyes were turned on me!

I cried out. I reached for the door and opened it. By the light of the moon, I saw the broken fence! The horses plunged through the opening and went over the cliff. The coach tumbled down with a mighty crash. Then everything went dark.

It seemed as though years had gone by when I finally woke up from a very deep sleep. My wife was by the side of my bed. I learned that I had been thrown out of the coach. I had been saved from death by landing in a deep pile of snow in the valley below. A farmer found me there when the sun came up. He took me to a doctor, who saved my life.

The accident took place *at the very same spot* where the mail coach went over the cliff nine years before!

I never told my wife what I have just told you. I did tell the doctor who took care of me. He looked at me in a funny way. Then he told me to rest and said I would soon feel better.

I often think about what that old scientist said. There are some things that science *cannot* explain. For I am sure of this. I *was* a passenger in that coach, twenty years ago! And I was traveling with three dead men!

L OOKING FOR FACTS IN THE STORY. How well can you find facts in a story? Put an *x* in the box next to the right answer.

1. How did the traveler get into the house?
   - ❏ a. Jacob let him in.
   - ❏ b. He forced his way in.
   - ❏ c. The scientist invited him in.

2. The old man said he had been living in the house for
   - ❏ a. thirteen years.
   - ❏ b. twenty years.
   - ❏ c. twenty-three years.

3. The fence near the sign was
   - ❏ a. broken.
   - ❏ b. new.
   - ❏ c. high.

4. The passengers in the coach
   - ❏ a. were friendly.
   - ❏ b. fell asleep.
   - ❏ c. did not say a word.

E XAMINING VOCABULARY WORDS. Here are four vocabulary questions. Put an *x* in the box next to the right answer. The vocabulary words are printed in **boldface** in the story. You may look back at the words before you answer the questions.

1. He was weary because he had been walking all day. The word *weary* means
   - ❏ a. tired.
   - ❏ b. foolish.
   - ❏ c. proud.

2. He saw a speck of light in the dark. The word *speck* means
   - ❏ a. a tiny bit.
   - ❏ b. a small hill.
   - ❏ c. a shadow.

3. He said, "I would cling to your boat if I were drowning." The word *cling* means
   - ❏ a. break.
   - ❏ b. go away from.
   - ❏ c. hold on to.

4. He shivered in the cold. The word *shivered* means
   - ❏ a. screamed.
   - ❏ b. shook.
   - ❏ c. stared.

	x **5** =	
NUMBER CORRECT		YOUR SCORE

	x **5** =	
NUMBER CORRECT		YOUR SCORE

A
DDING WORDS TO A PARAGRAPH.
Complete the paragraph below. Fill in each blank with one of the words in the box. Each word appears in the story. There are five words and four blanks, so one word in the box will not be used.

From 1860 to 1861, some United States _____ was carried by the "pony express."

1

Young riders on horses rode as fast as they could for 75

_____ . Then

2

_____ riders on

3

horses carried the mail another 75 miles. This continued until the entire _____ ,

4

nearly 2,000 miles, was covered.

| fresh | mail | distance |
| pleasant | miles |

R
EADING BETWEEN THE LINES.
These questions will help you think critically. You will have to think about what happened in the story, and then figure out the answers. Put an *x* in the box next to the right answer.

1. We may infer (figure out) that the old man decided to live alone because he
   - ❑ a. loved the woods.
   - ❑ b. wanted to get away from a world that laughed at him.
   - ❑ c. wanted to read books.

2. The story suggests that the passengers in the coach were
   - ❑ a. young men.
   - ❑ b. friends of the scientist.
   - ❑ c. ghosts.

3. Why did the doctor look at the traveler in a funny way?
   - ❑ a. His story was so strange.
   - ❑ b. The doctor was very tired.
   - ❑ c. The traveler seemed sad.

4. Which was true of the scientist?
   - ❑ a. He had many visitors.
   - ❑ b. He liked to travel.
   - ❑ c. He studied "spirits and ghosts."

[ ] x **5** = [ ]

NUMBER CORRECT   **YOUR SCORE**

[ ] x **5** = [ ]

NUMBER CORRECT   **YOUR SCORE**

N OTING STORY ELEMENTS.

Some story elements are **plot, character, setting,** and **mood**. Put an *x* in the box next to the right answer.

1. What happened last in the *plot*?
   - ❏ a. The traveler sat down in the coach.
   - ❏ b. The old man said the traveler could stay.
   - ❏ c. The traveler saw a man carrying a lantern.

2. Who is the *main character* in the story?
   - ❏ a. the old man
   - ❏ b. Jacob
   - ❏ c. the traveler, James Murray

3. The *mood* of the story is
   - ❏ a. funny.
   - ❏ b. frightening.
   - ❏ c. sad.

4. Which sentence tells the *theme* of the story?
   - ❏ a. A traveler gets lost.
   - ❏ b. An old man asks for news about the world.
   - ❏ c. A man tells about strange events that cannot be explained.

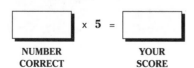

	x 5 =	
NUMBER CORRECT		**YOUR SCORE**

THINKING MORE ABOUT THE STORY. Your teacher might want you to write your answers

- ◆ Why didn't James Murray tell his wife about what happened to him? Give at least two reasons.
- ◆ Scientists read the old man's book. Then they called him a fool and laughed at him. What do you think the old man wrote?
- ◆ Many strange things take place in "The Mail Coach Road." List as many as you can.

Use the boxes below to total your scores for the exercises. Then write your score on pages 136 and 137.

	L OOKING FOR FACTS IN THE STORY
+	
	E XAMINING VOCABULARY WORDS
+	
	A DDING WORDS TO A PARAGRAPH
+	
	R EADING BETWEEN THE LINES
+	
	N OTING STORY ELEMENTS
▼	
	SCORE TOTAL: Story 7

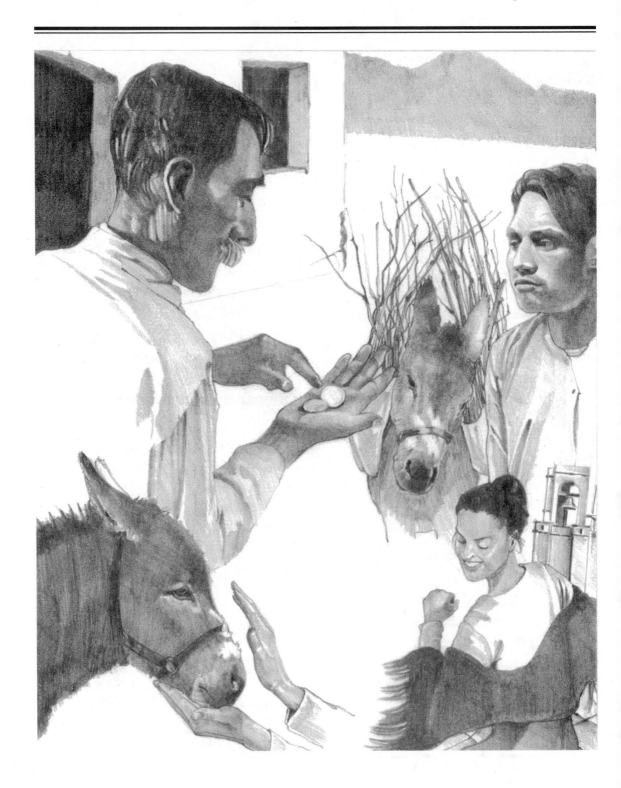

8

Ortega's Fortune

by Manuela Williams Crosno

Two things were close to Nicacio Ortega's heart. One was his donkey, Tino. The other was the place he called home.

Tino's coat was light gray. His eyes were large and dark. His nose was as black as the desert sky at night. He had one white foot and one white ear. And his playful heart was filled with mischief. He was always getting into and out of trouble.

Tino and Ortega spent much time together. They wandered through the forest, day after day, gathering wood to sell in Santa Fe.

Ortega's second love was his *casa*,[1] his home. It was nothing more than a hut on the side of a hill. But Ortega had built it with his own hands, and he loved it dearly. Inside the hut, a few pieces of old furniture stood on the earth, which served as the floor. There were also some heavy blankets to sleep on.

Ortega was a friendly young man. His eyes always seemed to sparkle with joy. His wife, Tomasita, scolded him often. But not even that could **disturb** the pleasant look on his face.

As for Tomasita, to tell the truth, she was very lazy. As soon as Ortega was out of sight, she hurried down the road. Then she spent the day **gossiping** with her neighbor, Señora Griego. Tomasita was very jealous of the Griegos. They lived in a house with four large rooms. Señor Griego worked in a mine. He earned much more money than Ortega, who was just a poor woodcutter.

---

1. casa: the Spanish word for "house."

Every day, Tomasita rushed back to her house. She got there before Ortega returned from work. She pretended to be very busy. She began to milk the goat. Then she prepared the dinner. She always greeted her husband with angry words.

"Where have you been all day?" she would complain. "Why did I leave my father's house to be so poor? Why do you not work in a mine like Señor Griego? You must stop selling wood and dig for coal."

Then she would push a plate of food at her husband.

Ortega said very little. He knew that he and his wife were poor. It was true that Tomasita came from a home that was also poor. But Ortega said nothing about that. He liked being a woodcutter. He liked the woods and the fields and the desert sky at night. Sometimes, when he worked until dark and was far from home, he built a small fire and slept under the stars. He listened to the coyotes call. He let the cries of the birds put him to sleep.

One day Ortega tied Tino to a post in the Plaza at Santa Fe. Ortega joined a group of woodcutters. He listened to a story that one of them was telling.

Tino used his nose to push the rope off the post. Then he walked quietly away. He quickly disappeared down one of the winding, dusty roads that led away from the Plaza.

Ortega soon discovered that Tino was gone. All of the woodcutters began talking at once. Each had a different idea about where Tino had gone. Finally the noisy group went off together down one of the streets.

Tino wandered to a part of the town where many artists live. The donkey stopped at a lovely white adobe house.[2] He ate a few flowers off the fence. The gate was open, so he walked into the yard.

In the yard stood a painting that had just been finished. It showed trees on the side of a mountain in the middle of October. The bright colors glowed in the afternoon sun.

---

2. adobe house: a house made of clay.

Tino was not one to admire a painting, no matter how beautiful. But the smell of the oils made Tino very curious. He brushed his nose against the painting. The painting fell to the ground. It lay there in the sand. Tino pressed his nose against the oils. Soon Tino's face was covered with paint.

Suddenly there was a loud cry. A man came running out of the house. He began shouting at Tino. The frightened donkey jumped back. A few sticks of wood fell off Tino's back onto the ground.

Just then Ortega and the other woodcutters appeared at the gate. They saw the angry artist pick up a piece of wood and rush at the donkey, ready to strike him.

Ortega ran forward to protect Tino. The artist realized then that the donkey must belong to that man. He turned and ran toward Ortega with the stick held high.

Suddenly a loud voice called out, "Stop that, Carlos! *Stop that at once!*" The artist paused with the stick still in the air.

A man had come out of the house next door. He was tall and well built. He had deep brown eyes. The man looked serious. But he also seemed amused.

The artist was very surprised. He did not think that anyone lived in the house next door. He wondered, "Who is this man? How does he know my name?"

"Your painting is ruined," said the man. "How much do you think it was worth?"

The artist thought for a while. "One hundred dollars!" he finally announced.

The man reached into his pocket and took out some money. He counted out the bills. "Here is one hundred dollars," he said. "Please take the money."

The artist could hardly speak. He took the money and went back into his house.

Ortega was amazed. He knew that rich visitors sometimes came to Santa Fe. But one hundred dollars! It seemed like a fortune to Ortega.

As the other woodcutters wandered away, Ortega turned to Tino. Ortega muttered softly, "Just look at you now! You are covered with paint. Tino, poor Tino. You are always getting into trouble."

The tall man interrupted. "How much do you want for your wood?" he asked.

"The wood is fifty cents," Ortega answered.

The man reached into his pocket a second time. He removed a silver dollar. "Here, take this," he said. "Keep the dollar. I do not want any change."

Ortega began to unload the wood.

"Never mind," said the man. "You may keep the wood."

Ortega could not believe his ears! Never before had anyone paid him more for his wood than he had asked! Never before had anyone bought wood without taking it! He had to hurry home to tell Tomasita!

Ortega arrived home at a very late hour.

"Where have you been wasting your time?" Tomasita asked, angrily.

Ortega did not answer at first. He walked to the table. By the light of the candle, he showed Tomasita the silver dollar. Tomasita seized it. Then she listened while Ortega told her what had happened.

When Ortega finished speaking, Tomasita said, "Now you shall sleep. In the morning go back to that man. This time ask him for a dollar for the wood."

"I cannot do that!" Ortega said. But Tomasita would give him no peace until he agreed to go.

The next day Ortega went with Tino to Santa Fe. He followed the street to the house where the tall man lived. Ortega knocked softly on the door. The man appeared.

"Will . . . will you buy my wood?" Ortega asked.

The man smiled at Ortega. "How much money do you want for it this time?" he asked.

Ortega paused. He was afraid to answer. But he thought about how angry Tomasita would be. "One dollar," he said.

"Very well," said the man. He reached into his pocket. Then he gave Ortega two silver dollars. And once again he refused to take any wood.

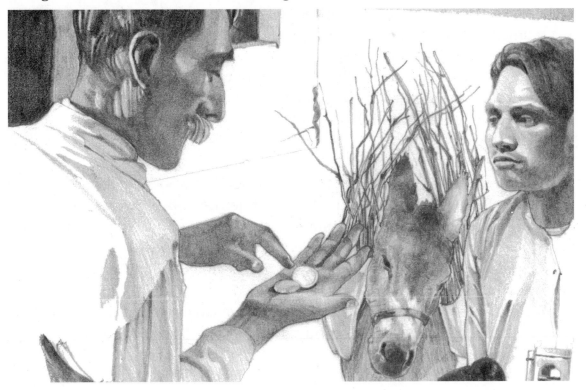

Ortega returned home pleased. But this was only because he had satisfied Tomasita's demand.

Tomasita met him at the door. When she saw the wood on Tino's back, she began to scream. "You did not find the man! You did not sell him the wood!"

Ortega held out the two silver dollars. Tomasita grabbed the coins. She turned them over in her hands. They gleamed in the light.

She said, "You shall sleep until morning. Then you must go back to that man again. This time ask him for *two* dollars for the wood."

Ortega refused. "I cannot do that!" he said. "He has already given me three dollars. And he has taken no wood! I cannot go back to the man again!"

"What?" shrieked his wife. "You will do what I say!" And she screamed until Ortega said he would go.

Day after day, Tomasita insisted that Ortega return to the man. Each time Ortega asked for one dollar more than he had asked for the day before. And each time the man gave Ortega twice as much money as Ortega asked for. But the man never took any wood.

Before very long, Tomasita had more than two thousand dollars. Most of the money was in bills. She kept them in an old jewel box that once belonged to her grandmother. She hid the box under the blanket on which she slept.

One day Ortega left for Santa Fe with his load of wood. As soon as he was gone, Tomasita hurried to the house of her neighbor, Señora Griego.

"We are going to move into a fine house," boasted Tomasita. "I will have many dresses made of silk. I will have maids to serve me."

Señora Griego said nothing. But her smile seemed to say, "I do not believe you."

When the unhappy Ortega came home, Tomasita grabbed the money he held in his hands. She said, "Do you remember the house of Señor Cordova where I worked as a girl?"

Ortega remembered the fine old house.

Tomasita said, "The house is for sale! Tomorrow I will buy it!"

Ortega begged his wife not to do that. He no longer spent any time in the forest or under the desert sky. And now Tomasita was going to make him move away from the house he loved. Some day she might even make him get rid of Tino!

Tomasita seemed to be reading Ortega's mind. She said, "You will not haul wood much longer. Then there will be no reason to keep that old donkey! You are going to be a gentleman! Do you hear?"

Early the next morning, Ortega was getting ready to go to Santa Fe. He was surprised to find that Tomasita was already up.

She said, "I will buy the Cordova house today! Meet me back here at six o'clock. I will take you to my new house then. Now bring your wood to the man in Santa Fe!"

It was *fiesta* day in the Plaza—a holiday. The Plaza was filled with crowds of people. There were bright colors and beautiful sounds. Food, music, and dancing were everywhere.

Tomasita had once loved to dance more than anything else. As she walked through the Plaza, an old friend, Ana, called out to her. "How are you, Tomasita? Come and dance with us."

"I will," said Tomasita. "But you must hold my jewel box." And she gave Ana the box that was filled with money.

Someone in the circle of dancers grabbed Tomasita's hand. A few minutes later, Ana wanted to dance. She put the box on top of a step where she thought she could watch it. Then she joined the dancers.

When Tomasita saw Ana dancing, she cried out in alarm, "Where is my jewel box!"

"There it is on the step," said Ana, pointing to the box. Tomasita rushed to the box and opened it **hastily.** But the box was empty! The money was gone!

Ortega walked slowly along the road that he knew so well. He wished he did not have to face the friendly man who kept giving him money. Finally Ortega found himself in front of the artist's house. Ortega looked around. He was amazed! Next to it was no other house! Both the house and the man had disappeared!

That evening, Tomasita was strangely silent. She did not even ask Ortega to give her the money. Tomasita had spent the whole day thinking. She finally told Ortega what had happened.

She said softly, "Nicacio. I am going back to the house of my mother and father. I go to **seek** a different life. Who knows what the future will bring?"

Ortega did not know then that his wife would change. He did not know then that she would return one day. He did not know then that she would bring him much love.

Ortega was still thinking about the tall man who had changed their lives. He was thinking about how he had suddenly appeared. And disappeared. It was strange, all so strange. Or was it?

LOOKING FOR FACTS IN THE STORY.
How well can you find facts in a story? Put an *x* in the box next to the right answer.

1. Señor Griego worked
   - ❏ a. as an artist.
   - ❏ b. as a woodcutter.
   - ❏ c. in a mine.

2. The tall man gave the artist
   - ❏ a. exactly fifty dollars.
   - ❏ b. one hundred dollars.
   - ❏ c. two hundred dollars.

3. Tomasita said she was going to buy
   - ❏ a. new furniture.
   - ❏ b. beautiful paintings.
   - ❏ c. a house.

4. What did Tomasita do with the jewel box?
   - ❏ a. She gave it to Ana.
   - ❏ b. She gave it to Ortega.
   - ❏ c. She put it on a step.

EXAMINING VOCABULARY WORDS.
Here are four vocabulary questions. Put an *x* in the box next to the right answer. The vocabulary words are printed in **boldface** in the story. You may look back at the words before you answer the questions.

1. Nothing seemed to disturb the pleasant look on his face. The word *disturb* means
   - ❏ a. change.
   - ❏ b. help.
   - ❏ c. enjoy.

2. She was gossiping with a friend. The word *gossiping* means
   - ❏ a. working very hard.
   - ❏ b. singing and dancing.
   - ❏ c. talking about others.

3. She rushed to the box and opened it hastily. The word *hastily* means
   - ❏ a. slowly.
   - ❏ b. quickly.
   - ❏ c. quietly.

4. She said, "I go to seek a different life." The word *seek* means
   - ❏ a. look for.
   - ❏ b. forget about.
   - ❏ c. remember.

	x 5 =	
NUMBER CORRECT		YOUR SCORE

	x 5 =	
NUMBER CORRECT		YOUR SCORE

A
DDING WORDS TO A PARAGRAPH. Complete the paragraph below. Fill in each blank with one of the words in the box. Each word appears in the story. There are five words and four blanks, so one word in the box will not be used.

Every summer, thousands of

_____ go to

1

Santa Fe, New Mexico. During

_____ weekends,

2

the Plaza in town is the center

of the good times. Bands play.

There are parties with singing and

_____ . And

3

interesting foods of all kinds are on

_____ everywhere.

4

holiday	wandering	sale
visitors	dancing	

	× **5** =	
NUMBER CORRECT		**YOUR SCORE**

R
EADING BETWEEN THE LINES. These questions will help you think critically. You will have to think about what happened in the story, and then figure out the answers. Put an *x* in the box next to the right answer.

1. Which sentence is true?
   - ❑ a. Happiness was more important than money to Ortega.
   - ❑ b. Ortega hated his house.
   - ❑ c. Tomasita never boasted.

2. An unusual thing about the tall man was that he
   - ❑ a. was quiet and shy.
   - ❑ b. lived next door to an artist.
   - ❑ c. paid a lot of money for wood he didn't take.

3. Tomasita was *not* planning to
   - ❑ a. buy dresses made of silk.
   - ❑ b. let Ortega keep Tino.
   - ❑ c. have many maids.

4. Which is true of Tomasita?
   - ❑ a. She liked Tino.
   - ❑ b. She finally found the money she lost.
   - ❑ c. Later, she went back to Ortega.

	× **5** =	
NUMBER CORRECT		**YOUR SCORE**

N OTING STORY ELEMENTS.

Some story elements are **plot, character, setting,** and **mood**. Put an *x* in the box next to the right answer.

1. What happened last in the *plot*?
   - ❑ a. Tomasita joined the dancers in the Plaza.
   - ❑ b. The man gave Ortega a silver dollar.
   - ❑ c. The artist picked up a stick and ran toward Tino.

2. Which sentence *characterizes* Tomasita?
   - ❑ a. She spent the whole day working very hard.
   - ❑ b. She was lazy and often yelled at Ortega.
   - ❑ c. She was very happy with her life.

3. The story is *set*
   - ❑ a. on a farm in California.
   - ❑ b. in a small town in France.
   - ❑ c. in and around Santa Fe.

4. The *mood* of the story is
   - ❑ a. funny.
   - ❑ b. scary.
   - ❑ c. serious.

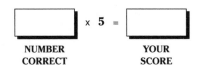

x **5** =

NUMBER CORRECT   YOUR SCORE

THINKING MORE ABOUT THE STORY. Your teacher might want you to write your answers.

- ◆ What were some of the things that Ortega loved? Think of as many as you can.
- ◆ At the end of the story, Ortega thought about the stranger. What might Ortega have been thinking? How did the man change their lives?
- ◆ Why do you think Tomasita went back to her parents' house? What lesson or lessons does the story teach?

Use the boxes below to total your scores for the exercises. Then write your score on pages 136 and 137.

L **OOKING FOR FACTS IN THE STORY**

+

E **XAMINING VOCABULARY WORDS**

+

A **DDING WORDS TO A PARAGRAPH**

+

R **EADING BETWEEN THE LINES**

+

N **OTING STORY ELEMENTS**

▼

SCORE TOTAL: Story 8

9

The Strange Orchid

by H. G. Wells

William Wellington was a quiet young man. He lived in a cottage at the edge of a woods. Years ago, the cottage belonged to his parents. After they died, they left it to him. William's parents also left him some money. It was just enough for William to live on.

Almost nothing in life interested William. He might have collected stamps. He might have saved coins. He might have read books. But he didn't care for those things. There was only one thing that William liked. He liked to grow orchids. Orchids are very lovely plants. Their flowers are known for their beautiful colors.

William always complained, "Nothing ever happens to me. All kinds of things happen to people I know. They always tell me about their adventures. But nothing interesting ever happens to me."

One day William was eating lunch with his housekeeper, Julia. William said to Julia, "I have a feeling that something is going to happen today. I just have that feeling. I feel that today is the day!"

"Oh, please don't say *that*," Julia said. She thought that "something happening" meant something that was bad.

"Don't worry," said William. "I don't mean anything bad."

William thought for a moment. Then he said, "I think that I'll go into the city today. The Peterson Company is having a sale. They're selling orchids that come from Africa. One of them may grow into a *new* kind of orchid. That would make me famous!"

William smiled. "That may be it! That may be the thing that will happen today!"

"From Africa?" said Julia. "Are those the orchids collected by that poor fellow you told me about? The man named Barton? The one who died in the jungle?"

"Yes," said William. He took a bite out of his sandwich. "You know, nothing exciting ever happens to me. All sorts of things happen to other people. Take Harvey, for example. Last Monday he found twenty dollars. On Wednesday his cat had six kittens. On Friday his cousin arrived suddenly from Australia. And on Saturday he fell and broke both of his legs."

"You could do without all that excitement," said Julia. "It can't be good. Look at what happened to Barton."

"Yes! That's it exactly!" exclaimed William. "Look at what happened to Barton! He was only thirty-six when he died. But he had already been married twice. Four times he was sick with a fever so high, he was close to death. He broke his arm once. And he died in the jungle collecting those orchids the Peterson Company is selling. His life was so *interesting*!"

William looked at his watch. "It's one o'clock now. The train leaves at two. I'll be able to get to the station in plenty of time."

His housekeeper said, "If you are going to the city, take an umbrella. It looks like it might rain."

When William returned, he was very happy. He had bought three small orchids. They were mostly roots. He put them down on the table. Then he told his housekeeper about them.

William said, "As soon as I saw these, I bought them at once. They're small, of course. So it's hard to know how they'll **actually** turn out. But I liked the way they look."

William smiled. "I *knew* that something would happen today. I just know that one of these orchids will be special! I can feel it in my heart."

William pointed to the smallest of the three. He said, "I've never seen an orchid like this one before. It may be a new kind. This was one of the last orchids that Barton collected."

"I don't like the way it looks," said his housekeeper. "I think that it's ugly. I don't like those things that stick out. The whole plant looks like a spider pretending to be dead."

William looked again at the root. "Well," he said. "It may not look pretty to you now. But you never can tell how these things will grow. It may turn out to be a very beautiful orchid. I'll plant it tomorrow."

William started to leave. Then he turned and said, "Oh. They found Barton lying dead in a swamp in the jungle. An orchid was found crushed right under his body. He had been sick for a few days, it seems. I suppose he became weak and fainted. They found *two deep red lines* around Barton's neck. A snake wrapped itself around him, I guess."

Julia was shocked. "Imagine!" she said. "Dying alone in a swamp in a jungle!"

"It couldn't have been fun," William said. Then his face brightened. "But Barton died doing what he liked! Anyway, it makes these plants more interesting. Don't you think so?"

The next few days were very busy ones for William. He worked in the green-house behind his cottage. He planted the roots. He watered them often.

Two of the orchids died. But the third one—the smallest— began to grow nicely.

William called Julia into the green-house. He showed her the plant. "That is a bud," he said. "Soon there will be leaves. Hmnnnn. Those things on the plant—they look like vines."

"I don't like them," said Julia. "They're like fingers reaching out."

"That is a little strange," William said. "I have never seen vines like those on an orchid. Perhaps this *is* a new kind of orchid. I may yet become famous."

"Anyhow, I don't like it," said the housekeeper. And she left the greenhouse.

William felt a little hurt that Julia didn't like the plant. But he cared for the orchid. It continued to grow.

One day the leaves began to appear. They were dark green with red spots. William had never seen leaves like those before. He said to Julia, "Come and look at the leaves."

"Thank you," she said. "But I'd rather not go. The greenhouse is hot. It gives me a headache." She had seen the plant before. The vines were *very* long and thick. She had never liked the way they looked. Now they scared her a little.

Finally, the great day arrived! As soon as William entered the greenhouse, he knew that the orchid had bloomed! A rich, sweet smell filled the air. William rushed to look at the orchid. He saw that it had three large flowers. They were purple and white mixed with orange and gold. William was delighted! He could tell that this was a new kind of orchid.

As William stood next to the orchid, he suddenly felt strange. The smell was very sweet. And the greenhouse was so hot. Then everything seemed to spin around and around. William felt weak and dropped to the ground.

At 4:30 the housekeeper made tea. But William did not come in, as he usually did.

Julia said to herself, "He must be in the greenhouse. He is probably looking at his special orchid. I will go and get him."

She went to the greenhouse. She opened the door and called his name. There was no answer. She noticed that the air was very hot and that it smelled very sweet.

Then she saw William lying on the ground. He was lying next to the orchid. The vines from the orchid had reached out! Two of the vines were wrapped around William's neck. They were choking him to death! Other vines were wrapped around his arms.

Julia cried out and ran to William's side. She tried to pull the vines away from his neck. The vines were as tight as ropes. But her hands were stronger than she knew. Using all her strength, she finally snapped the two vines. Then she stared in horror at William's neck. Around his neck she saw *two deep red lines!*

The strong smell of the orchid made Julia's head spin. But she knew she must not faint. She picked up a flowerpot. She **hurled** it through the greenhouse window. Cool air flowed in, and Julia felt better.

Julia looked around. On a shelf nearby, she saw string and a knife. She picked up the knife. Then one by one she cut through the vines until William was free.

A neighbor was hurrying along the path to the greenhouse. He had heard the glass break and wondered what was the matter. The man was amazed to see Julia dragging William away from the greenhouse.

"Quickly!" she shouted. "Go and get Dr. Hadley!"

William opened his eyes. "What's the matter?" he said weakly.

"You fainted in the greenhouse."

"And the orchid?" he asked.

"I will take care of that!" Julia answered firmly.

Luckily, William was not badly hurt. The doctor ordered him to rest in bed for two days. Then Julia told the doctor what had happened. "Come to the greenhouse and see," she said.

Cold air was blowing in through the window. The sweet smell was gone.

"There," said Julia, pointing to the orchid.

The plant was dying. But as the doctor came near, one of its vines suddenly reached out toward him. The doctor **shuddered** and hurried away.

The next morning the strange orchid was dead. It lay in a **heap** on the greenhouse floor. But upstairs, William was bright and lively. He had never been so happy. He could not stop thinking about his adventure. Something exciting had happened to him at last!

LOOKING FOR FACTS IN THE STORY.

How well can you find facts in a story? Put an *x* in the box next to the right answer.

1. The only thing that William liked was
   - ❑ a. saving coins.
   - ❑ b. growing orchids.
   - ❑ c. collecting stamps.

2. William complained that
   - ❑ a. he didn't have enough money.
   - ❑ b. his friends weren't interesting.
   - ❑ c. nothing ever happened to him.

3. Julia thought that the orchid
   - ❑ a. was ugly.
   - ❑ b. was very lovely.
   - ❑ c. cost too much money.

4. At the end of the story, William felt
   - ❑ a. scared.
   - ❑ b. badly hurt.
   - ❑ c. very happy.

EXAMINING VOCABULARY WORDS.

Here are four vocabulary questions. Put an *x* in the box next to the right answer. The vocabulary words are printed in **boldface** in the story. You may look back at the words before you answer the questions.

1. He didn't actually know how the orchid would turn out. The word *actually* means
   - ❑ a. really.
   - ❑ b. foolishly.
   - ❑ c. ever.

2. She hurled it through a window. The word *hurled* means
   - ❑ a. broke.
   - ❑ b. threw.
   - ❑ c. kicked.

3. The doctor shuddered and hurried away. The word *shuddered* means
   - ❑ a. enjoyed seeing.
   - ❑ b. shouted at.
   - ❑ c. shook with fear.

4. It lay in a heap on the floor. The word *heap* means
   - ❑ a. pile.
   - ❑ b. dirt.
   - ❑ c. rock.

	x 5 =	
NUMBER CORRECT		**YOUR SCORE**

	x 5 =	
NUMBER CORRECT		**YOUR SCORE**

ADDING WORDS TO A PARAGRAPH.
Complete the paragraph below. Fill in each blank with one of the words in the box. Each word appears in the story. There are five words and four blanks, so one word in the box will not be used.

Many people believe that

_____ are
₁

the most beautiful flowers in

the world. Orchids can grow

_____ except
₂

in the coldest spots. However,

the most _____
₃

orchids grow in very hot places.

Most of the orchids sold in

flower shops have been raised in a

_____ .
₄

| anywhere | orchids | excitement |
| greenhouse | lovely | |

| | x **5** = | |
| NUMBER CORRECT | | YOUR SCORE |

READING BETWEEN THE LINES.
These questions will help you think critically. You will have to think about what happened in the story, and then figure out the answers. Put an *x* in the box next to the right answer.

1. We may infer (figure out) that the new kind of orchid
   - ❑ a. did not have any flowers.
   - ❑ b. was like most orchids.
   - ❑ c. killed Barton.

2. Which sentence is true?
   - ❑ a. William was never in any real danger.
   - ❑ b. Julia was right to be scared by the plant.
   - ❑ c. William once broke his leg.

3. William fainted because
   - ❑ a. he hadn't eaten all day.
   - ❑ b. the smell of the orchid was so sweet and so strong.
   - ❑ c. the orchid looked so beautiful.

4. It is fair to say that Julia
   - ❑ a. saved William's life.
   - ❑ b. was very weak.
   - ❑ c. didn't care about William.

| | x **5** = | |
| NUMBER CORRECT | | YOUR SCORE |

N OTING STORY ELEMENTS.

Some story elements are **plot, character, setting,** and **mood.** Put an *x* in the box next to the right answer.

1. What happened first in the *plot*?
   - ❑ a. William fell to the floor.
   - ❑ b. Julia cut the vines.
   - ❑ c. William bought three small orchids.

2. What was most important in the *plot*?
   - ❑ a. The doctor told William to rest for two days.
   - ❑ b. William didn't come for tea, as he usually did.
   - ❑ c. Harvey's cousin arrived suddenly from Australia.

3. Which sentence *characterizes* William?
   - ❑ a. He was a quiet young man with few interests.
   - ❑ b. He had many adventures.
   - ❑ c. He lived in the country.

4. Where is the story *set*?
   - ❑ a. in a jungle in Africa
   - ❑ b. at the Peterson Company
   - ❑ c. in a cottage and a green-house

[ ] x **5** = [ ]

NUMBER CORRECT   **YOUR SCORE**

THINKING MORE ABOUT THE STORY.
Your teacher might want you to write your answers.

◆ William had a strong feeling that something important would happen to him that day. Was William right? Explain.

◆ Julia saw two deep red lines around William's neck. Tell why that was important.

◆ What things were strange or unusual about the new orchid? List as many as you can. Which of these suggest that the orchid could cause harm?

Use the boxes below to total your scores for the exercises. Then write your score on pages 136 and 137.

[ ]   **L** OOKING FOR FACTS IN THE STORY
+
[ ]   **E** XAMINING VOCABULARY WORDS
+
[ ]   **A** DDING WORDS TO A PARAGRAPH
+
[ ]   **R** EADING BETWEEN THE LINES
+
[ ]   **N** OTING STORY ELEMENTS
▼
[ ]   **SCORE TOTAL:** Story 9

10

Watch Out!

by Bruce Coville

I'm home," yelled Kirby Markle. He burst through the front door of his house. Without waiting for an answer, he ran up the stairs and dashed into his bedroom. He dropped down onto his bed. Then he tore open the box he had bought at that strange store he found when he took the new shortcut home.

Inside he found a second box. "THE CAVE OF THE GNOME," stated bold, black letters written across the top.

Beneath, in smaller print, it said, "Fool Your Family! Amaze Your Friends! A Great Trick For Magicians Young And Old."

Kirby examined the box with wide eyes. Maybe this would finally be the trick he got to work. The old man who had sold it to him said it was made just for someone like him, who was in a hurry to learn magic.

Kirby tore open the flaps that held the box shut. He held the box upside down over his bed.

Out tumbled a cave made of papier-mâché.[1]

A look of **doubt** crossed Kirby's face. He couldn't see any way that this was going to make things disappear.

"Kirby! Supper!"

Kirby sighed. He really didn't want to go to supper now. He wanted to figure out how to make this trick work.

"Just a minute, Mom!"

He began reading the directions.

"Kirby!"

---

1. papier-mâché: a mix of paper and glue that becomes hard when it dries.

"All right, all right. I'm coming!" Kirby shoved the directions into his pocket and rushed down the stairs.

As soon as supper was over, Kirby asked his mother and father to come into the living room. "I have something I want to show you," he said.

He led them through the door and onto the couch. Then he raced back upstairs to grab the cave.

"I got a new trick today," he announced, as he hurried back down the steps, two and three at a time.

Kirby's parents exchanged smiles. Kirby wanted so badly to be a magician. But he had never yet gotten a trick to work. He was always so eager to show them off that he never took the time to learn how to do them right.

"Did you read the directions yet?" asked his mother.

"Sort of," said Kirby. "It's gonna be great. Now, I need something to put in the cave. Can I have your watch, Dad?"

Kirby's father looked worried. "Will I get it back?" he asked.

"Oh, Dad."

"Well, okay," said his father, smiling. "But be careful with it. It's quite expensive."

He took off his watch and gave it to Kirby.

"Now, watch this," said Kirby. He put the watch in the cave. Then he rolled the little papier-mâché **boulder** across the front of it. He put his right hand on the cave and read the magic words off the instruction sheet. At the same time he gave the top a little twist to the right. He smiled to himself. The twist must be what started the trick that would hide the watch.

BOOM!

The noise was so loud it shook the windows. A puff of smoke rose from the cave. Red flames shot out around the little boulder.

Kirby snatched his hand away. "Ow!" he cried.

Mr. and Mrs. Markle looked at each other nervously.

Trying to act calm, Kirby removed the boulder from the front of the cave.

The watch was gone.

"Presto kazam!" he said with a big smile. "A real magic trick!"

Kirby's parents clapped. But his father had a worried look on his face. "Why don't you bring the watch back now?" he said gently.

"You bet!" said Kirby. He put the boulder back in front of the cave and twisted the top to the left.

Nothing happened.

He tried it again.

Nothing happened.

He twisted it to the right.

Nothing happened.

Kirby grabbed the directions and began reading. Suddenly he turned very pale.

"What is it, Kirby?" asked his mother.

Without saying a word, Kirby handed her the paper.

Gregory Gnome was in his cave when he heard the bell ring. A greedy smile crossed his face. He ran to the loading platform.

The smile faded a little. Another gold watch. Well, it was better than a kick in the pants, he thought with a shrug. He tossed it into a box already filled with watches. He really would have to have a cave sale someday soon to turn some of this stuff into cash.

"Gregory!" said a voice behind him. "Aren't you **ashamed** of yourself, taking advantage of all those children?"

Gregory jumped. He pretended to look hurt. As he turned to his wife, he pulled a sheet of paper from his pocket. "Look at these directions," he said. "Read the last paragraph to me."

It was his wife's turn to sigh. "I don't have to read it," she said. "I know it by heart: 'Once something is placed in the Cave of the Gnome, it can never be returned. So please be sure to use only things that have no real value.'"

"Well, there it is," said Gregory. "It could hardly be any plainer, could it? All I wanted to do was give kids a toy they could have some fun with. Can I help it if not one out of twenty is smart enough to read the directions before trying to use the thing? Can I?"

Gregory tried to look serious. But he could not hide the greedy smile that **twitched** at the corners of his mouth.

The little papier-mâché cave was in tiny pieces all over Kirby's living room floor.

Of papier-mâché there was a lot. Of the gold watch, not a sign.

"Kirby," said Mr. Markle, "come with me. I want to have a little talk with you."

Slowly, very slowly, Kirby followed his father out of the room.

L OOKING FOR FACTS IN THE STORY.
How well can you find facts in a story? Put an *x* in the box next to the right answer.

1. The man at the store said the magic trick was
   - ❑ a. new.
   - ❑ b. hard to do.
   - ❑ c. just right for someone like Kirby.

2. What did Kirby put in the cave?
   - ❑ a. a toy
   - ❑ b. a watch
   - ❑ c. a box

3. The directions said that once something was put in the cave, it
   - ❑ a. could never be returned.
   - ❑ b. would be returned later.
   - ❑ c. might get broken.

4. Who ended up with the gold watch?
   - ❑ a. Kirby
   - ❑ b. Kirby's father
   - ❑ c. Gregory Gnome

E XAMINING VOCABULARY WORDS.
Here are four vocabulary questions. Put an *x* in the box next to the right answer. The vocabulary words are printed in **boldface** in the story. You may look back at the words before you answer the questions.

1. A look of doubt was on his face. When you are in *doubt,* you are
   - ❑ a. not sure.
   - ❑ b. certain.
   - ❑ c. filled with joy.

2. He rolled the little boulder in front of the cave. A *boulder* is
   - ❑ a. a wheel.
   - ❑ b. a rock.
   - ❑ c. a gate.

3. He should be ashamed of what he did. You are *ashamed* when you have done something
   - ❑ a. wrong.
   - ❑ b. right.
   - ❑ c. easily.

4. A smile twitched at the corners of his mouth. The word *twitched* means
   - ❑ a. hurt.
   - ❑ b. stared.
   - ❑ c. moved.

	x 5 =	
NUMBER CORRECT		**YOUR SCORE**

	x 5 =	
NUMBER CORRECT		**YOUR SCORE**

Complete the paragraph below. Fill in each blank with one of the words in the box. Each word appears in the story. There are five words and four blanks, so one word in the box will not be used.

Some of the world's earliest art has been found on the walls of

_____. Most of
₁

these cave paintings

_____ wild animals
₂

that were hunted long ago. The

most famous cave paintings are

_____ in France.
₃

But over the years, the colors on

these paintings have _____.
₄

eager	show	faded
caves	found	

These questions will help you think critically. You will have to think about what happened in the story, and then figure out the answers. Put an *x* in the box next to the right answer.

1. Kirby's mistake was that he didn't
   - ❏ a. begin to read the directions.
   - ❏ b. finish reading the directions.
   - ❏ c. understand the directions.

2. We may infer (figure out) that what happened to Kirby
   - ❏ a. never happened before.
   - ❏ b. happened once in a while.
   - ❏ c. often happened to kids.

3. How did Gregory Gnome feel at the end of the story?
   - ❏ a. very sorry
   - ❏ b. very angry
   - ❏ c. very pleased with himself

4. The last lines of the story suggest that Kirby's father was
   - ❏ a. unhappy with Kirby.
   - ❏ b. delighted by the trick.
   - ❏ c. not troubled by what had happened.

[____] x **5** = [____]

NUMBER   YOUR
CORRECT   SCORE

[____] x **5** = [____]

NUMBER   YOUR
CORRECT   SCORE

NOTING STORY ELEMENTS.

Some story elements are **plot, character, setting,** and **mood**. Put an *x* in the box next to the right answer.

1. What happened first in the *plot*?
   - ❑ a. Gregory Gnome heard the bell ringing.
   - ❑ b. Kirby read the magic words.
   - ❑ c. Mr. Markle asked Kirby to bring back the watch.

2. Which word *characterizes* Gregory Gnome?
   - ❑ a. kind
   - ❑ b. friendly
   - ❑ c. greedy

3. Where is the story *set*?
   - ❑ a. in a store that sells magic tricks
   - ❑ b. in a house and a cave
   - ❑ c. at a school

4. The *mood* of the story is
   - ❑ a. amusing.
   - ❑ b. very frightening.
   - ❑ c. very serious.

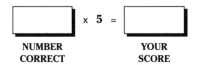

| NUMBER CORRECT | × 5 = | YOUR SCORE |

THINKING MORE ABOUT THE STORY. Your teacher might want you to write your answers.

◆ At one point, Kirby grabbed the directions and began reading. Then he turned pale. What do you think happened?

◆ Gregory said, "All I wanted to do was give kids a trick they would have some fun with." Do you believe him? Why?

◆ How do you think Gregory's wife felt about the trick? What lesson or lessons does "Watch Out!" teach?

Use the boxes below to total your scores for the exercises. Then write your score on pages 136 and 137.

☐	**L** OOKING FOR FACTS IN THE STORY
+	
☐	**E** XAMINING VOCABULARY WORDS
+	
☐	**A** DDING WORDS TO A PARAGRAPH
+	
☐	**R** EADING BETWEEN THE LINES
+	
☐	**N** OTING STORY ELEMENTS
▼	
☐	**SCORE TOTAL:** Story 10

11

Mrs. Mansley's View

by Edith Wharton

Mrs. Mansley lived alone in an apartment in New York City. Her husband had died many years ago. She did not have children.

Mrs. Mansley was not lonely at first. Now and then friends walked up the stairs to her room on the third floor. But as time went on, they stopped coming to visit.

Mrs. Mansley loved to sit by the window and look out. She loved the **view**. She could see trees and plants, butterflies and birds. She watched the flowers turn yellow, and pink, and white. She enjoyed looking at the yards—at the old brick walls and the brightly colored curtains. She liked watching the seasons as they changed. There were green buds in spring. There were trees without leaves on gray afternoons in winter.

She spent many hours sitting by the window. Sometimes she brought a book and read for a while. Then she would look out to see a neighbor planting flowers or painting a fence. Yes, Mrs. Mansley loved the view. It brought interest and beauty to her life.

One April day, Mrs. Mansley was sitting in her chair by the window. She was looking at the magnolia tree in the yard next door. The sky was blue. It was filled with white clouds. There was a knock on the door. A moment later, her landlady, Mrs. Simpson, entered the room.

"Ah, Mrs. Simpson," said Mrs. Mansley. "I see that the magnolia already has flowers this year."

"The what?" asked Mrs. Simpson. She looked around the room. She did not know what Mrs. Mansley was talking about.

"The magnolia tree in the yard next door. In Mrs. Blake's yard."

"Really?" said Mrs. Simpson. "I didn't know there was a tree in the yard."

Mrs. Mansley stared at Mrs. Simpson. She didn't know there was a tree in the yard next door! Mrs. Mansley had looked at that tree hundreds of times.

Mrs. Simpson said, "Speaking of Mrs. Blake, the work on her house will begin next week."

"The work?" It was Mrs. Mansley's turn to be surprised.

"Didn't you know? Mrs. Blake is going to add some new rooms to her house. The new rooms will go all the way across the yard. I don't see how she can **afford** to build something that big. Anyhow, the work will begin on Monday."

Mrs. Mansley had grown pale. She slowly asked, "Do you know how high the new rooms will be?"

"That's the ridiculous part. They'll be three floors high—as high as this building. Did you ever hear of such a thing!"

Mrs. Mansley said, "Won't that bother you very much, Mrs. Simpson?"

"I should say it will! But it seems she has the right to build it that high. So there's nothing I can do. Good day, Mrs. Mansley."

Mrs. Mansley turned to the window again. How lovely the view was that day! The blue sky with its white clouds cast a glow over everything. The magnolia certainly looked pretty that afternoon. But soon a high, wide wall

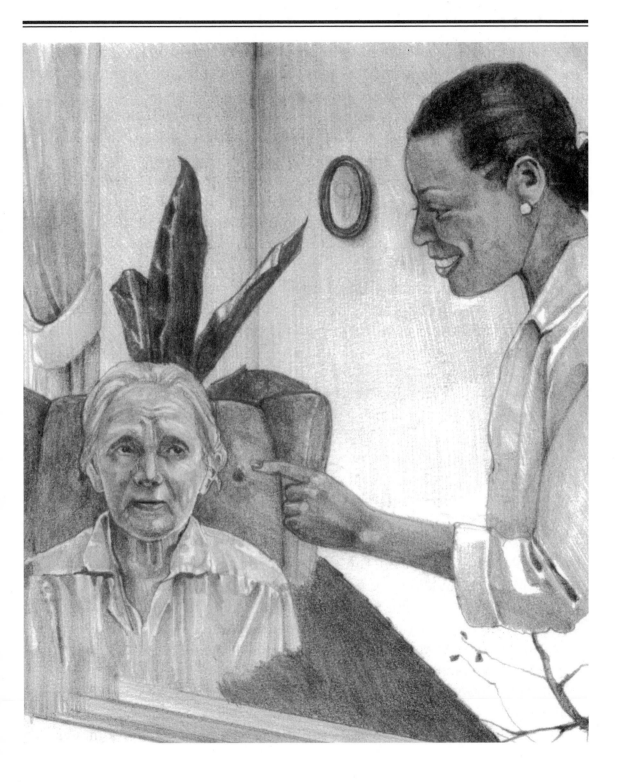

would rise up. Her view would be blocked! Everything would be hidden! Her world would disappear! Mrs. Mansley sat by the window until dark. She went to bed, but she could not sleep.

Early the next day, Mrs. Mansley got up and went to the window. It was raining and gray. She looked at Mrs. Blake's brick house with its old wooden porch. She shook her head.

"I might move," Mrs. Mansley said to herself. She turned from the window. She looked around the room. She might move, of course. But she was not likely to do that. She had lived in that place for seventeen years. She knew it very well. She was used to it. "I am too old to move," Mrs. Mansley said softly.

That afternoon the weather cleared. The sun forced its way through the clouds. The earth in the flower beds looked dark and rich. It was Thursday. On Monday the work on the house was to begin.

On Sunday, Mrs. Mansley went to Mrs. Blake's house. Mrs. Mansley introduced herself. Mrs. Blake invited her in.

"I am glad to meet you," Mrs. Blake said. "I understand that you live across the yard. I rent out rooms. My house is full right now. But I am adding new rooms. Perhaps you would like to move into one of those rooms next year."

"It is about those new rooms that I have come," Mrs. Mansley said. "I want to talk to you about those new rooms. I'll have to tell you something about myself first to make you understand."

Mrs. Blake was surprised. But she seemed ready to listen.

Mrs. Mansley said, "I have never been very happy. I never really got what I wanted, you see. For years I wanted to live in the country. I often dreamed about that. But we did not have enough money to move. Then my husband died and I was left alone. That was seventeen years ago. I went to stay at Mrs. Simpson's place. And I have been there ever since. I have grown older and weaker, as you can see. I don't go out very often. So sitting at my window means a great deal to me. My window—"

"Well, then," said Mrs. Blake, "I could give you a very nice room. One of the new rooms in back would—"

"But I *don't* want to move! I can't move!" said Mrs. Mansley, almost with a scream. "I came to say that if you build those new rooms, I shall have no view from my window. No view! *No view* from my window! Do you understand that?"

Mrs. Blake thought she must be talking to a woman who had gone mad.

"Dear me," she said softly. "That's bad, isn't it? Why I never thought about that. The new rooms *will* get in the way of your view, Mrs. Mansley."

"You *do* understand, then," said Mrs. Mansley."

"Why, *of course* I do. I am very sorry about it too. But don't you worry at all. I can take care of that."

Mrs. Blake tried to move Mrs. Mansley toward the door.

"I'm not rich," said Mrs. Mansley. "But I can give you some money, if that would help."

"There's no need to do that. Now you really must go. I'm very busy right now. There's so much I must do."

"But you haven't given me an answer," Mrs. Mansley said.

"Why, I'll think it over. I certainly will."

"But they say that the work will begin tomorrow!"

Mrs. Blake paused. "Well, it won't begin. I promise you that. I'll send word to the builder right after you leave."

"You're not just saying that, are you, Mrs. Blake?"

"No—no! How can you think such a thing," Mrs. Blake answered.

She held the door open. Mrs. Mansley went out.

"Well!" exclaimed Mrs. Blake. She closed and locked the door. "Who would have guessed that old lady was crazy? Who could have known that?"

Mrs. Mansley slept well that night. But she was awakened very early the next morning by the sound of loud voices. She got up. Then she went to the window and looked out. She saw workers in Mrs. Blake's yard. They were carrying lumber and bricks. Mrs. Mansley realized that Mrs. Blake had not told her the truth. Mrs. Mansley did not wish to see what was going on. With a heavy heart, she went back to bed.

But late in the afternoon, she went over to the window. She felt she must know the worst. She watched the workers as they did their job. They had torn down part of the wooden porch at the back of the building.

"Careful, Jim," called one of the men to another worker who was smoking a pipe. "If you throw matches near those papers, you'll have this old porch burning down before you know it."

Mrs. Mansley leaned forward. She saw some bundles of old newspapers next to the porch.

Not much later, the workers left. Mrs. Mansley sat at the window. She looked out until the sun set. Then she went to bed.

That night she could not sleep. The weather had changed. A wild wind was blowing. In the middle of the night she got up. She put on a thin coat. She found some matches. Then she slowly made her way down the dark stairs. She went outside. She was **chilled** by the wind as she walked through the yard with the matches in her hand.

At three o'clock that morning, a fire engine arrived at Mrs. Blake's building. The wooden porch at the back was on fire. Mrs. Mansley leaned out of her open window. As the cold wind swept into her room, she watched the flames.

The fire was quickly put out. No one was hurt. In fact, the person who **suffered** the most was Mrs. Mansley. In the morning she began to cough. She had trouble breathing. Mrs. Simpson sent for a doctor.

"She is sick—very, very sick," said the doctor. "She is too sick to be moved. I will send a nurse."

The next day Mrs. Mansley was very weak. The nurse asked Mrs. Simpson to come into the room. As they bent over the old woman, they saw her lips move.

"Lift me up—out of the bed," she whispered. She pointed to the window.

"She wants to sit near the window," Mrs. Simpson explained. "She used to sit there all day. I—I suppose it can do her no harm."

"Nothing matters now," the nurse said softly.

They carried Mrs. Mansley to the window and placed her in her chair. It was a beautiful day. The sun was shining. In Mrs. Blake's yard everything was quiet. The burned pieces of wood from the porch lay on the ground where they had fallen. Since the fire, the builders had not returned to their work.

It was hard for Mrs. Mansley to breathe. And each moment it grew harder. She tried to make them open the window, but they did not under-stand. She only wanted to feel the air. She was not able to do that. But the view—the view! The *view,* at least, was there!

Mrs. Mansley's head fell back, and she died with a smile on her face.

Later that day, the workers began to build again.

LOOKING FOR FACTS IN THE STORY.
How well can you find facts in a story? Put an *x* in the box next to the right answer.

1. From her window, Mrs. Mansley could see
   - ❑ a. trees and flowers.
   - ❑ b. stores and shops.
   - ❑ c. the top of mountains.

2. Mrs. Mansley had lived in the apartment for
   - ❑ a. nearly fifteen years.
   - ❑ b. seventeen years.
   - ❑ c. twenty years.

3. Mrs. Blake thought that Mrs. Mansley was
   - ❑ a. rich.
   - ❑ b. interesting.
   - ❑ c. mad.

4. Mrs. Blake promised that she would
   - ❑ a. rent a room to Mrs. Mansley.
   - ❑ b. visit Mrs. Mansley later.
   - ❑ c. tell the builder not to start work.

EXAMINING VOCABULARY WORDS.
Here are four vocabulary questions. Put an *x* in the box next to the right answer. The vocabulary words are printed in **boldface** in the story. You may look back at the words before you answer the questions.

1. She loved the view from her window. The word *view* means
   - ❑ a. things you can see.
   - ❑ b. friends and neighbors.
   - ❑ c. a cool breeze.

2. She didn't know how Mrs. Blake could afford to build so many rooms. The word *afford* means
   - ❑ a. tell people about.
   - ❑ b. have the money for.
   - ❑ c. begin very soon.

3. She was chilled by the wind. The word *chilled* means
   - ❑ a. knocked over.
   - ❑ b. made cold.
   - ❑ c. blown away.

4. Mrs. Mansley was the person who suffered the most from the fire. The word *suffered* means
   - ❑ a. was harmed.
   - ❑ b. was helped.
   - ❑ c. was forgotten.

	x 5 =	
NUMBER CORRECT		**YOUR SCORE**

	x 5 =	
NUMBER CORRECT		**YOUR SCORE**

A
DDING WORDS TO A PARAGRAPH. Complete the paragraph below. Fill in each blank with one of the words in the box. Each word appears in the story. There are five words and four blanks, so one word in the box will not be used.

Magnolia is the name of a

group of _____
₁

and trees. Magnolia trees are

known for their hard,

_____ wood.
₂

The _____ from
₃

the tree is used to make furniture.

Although most magnolia trees are

small, the largest ones grow more

than one _____
₄

feet tall.

hundred	lumber	seasons
beautiful		bushes

[ ] x **5** = [ ]

NUMBER   YOUR
CORRECT   SCORE

R
EADING BETWEEN THE LINES. These questions will help you think critically. You will have to think about what happened in the story, and then figure out the answers. Put an *x* in the box next to the right answer.

1. We may infer (figure out) that Mrs. Mansley
   - ❏ a. had many friends.
   - ❏ b. was going to move.
   - ❏ c. started the fire.

2. The new rooms were going to be built
   - ❏ a. at the front of Mrs. Blake's building.
   - ❏ b. in the garden.
   - ❏ c. where the porch was.

3. At first, Mrs. Mansley could not look at the workers because
   - ❏ a. it upset her too much.
   - ❏ b. she was very tired.
   - ❏ c. it was dark outside.

4. Which sentence is true?
   - ❏ a. Mrs. Blake told Mrs. Mansley the truth.
   - ❏ b. The cold wind made Mrs. Mansley sick.
   - ❏ c. Mrs. Mansley died in bed.

[ ] x **5** = [ ]

NUMBER   YOUR
CORRECT   SCORE

N OTING STORY ELEMENTS.
Some story elements are **plot, character, setting,** and **mood**. Put an *x* in the box next to the right answer.

1. What happened last in the *plot*?
   - ❑ a. Mrs. Mansley went to Mrs. Blake's house.
   - ❑ b. Mrs. Simpson said that Mrs. Blake was building new rooms.
   - ❑ c. They carried Mrs. Mansley to the chair by the window.

2. Who is the *main character* in the story?
   - ❑ a. Mrs. Simpson
   - ❑ b. Mrs. Mansley
   - ❑ c. Mrs. Blake

3. The story is *set*
   - ❑ a. in New York City.
   - ❑ b. in Chicago.
   - ❑ c. in San Francisco.

4. What is the *mood* of the story?
   - ❑ a. funny
   - ❑ b. scary
   - ❑ c. sad

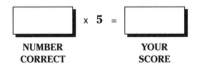

NUMBER CORRECT   x **5** =   YOUR SCORE

THINKING MORE ABOUT THE STORY.
Your teacher might want you to write your answers.

◆ Mrs. Mansley does not seem like the kind of person who would start a fire. Explain why she did.

◆ Suppose Mrs. Mansley had not heard a worker warn another about throwing matches near the porch. Do you think the story would have had a different ending? Discuss.

◆ Mrs. Manley died with a smile on her face. Explain why.

Use the boxes below to total your scores for the exercises. Then write your score on pages 136 and 137.

L OOKING FOR FACTS IN THE STORY

+

E XAMINING VOCABULARY WORDS

+

A DDING WORDS TO A PARAGRAPH

+

R EADING BETWEEN THE LINES

+

N OTING STORY ELEMENTS

▼

SCORE TOTAL: Story 11

12

For Better or Worse

by W. W. Jacobs

George Walters and Ben Davis were sailors. They had spent many years at sea. One afternoon, they met on the street. They sat down on a bench and began to talk.

Ben announced, "I've had a shock, George. I've heard news about my wife."

"I didn't know you were married," said George.

"We broke up," said Ben. "Thirty-five years ago. I went off to sea and never saw her again."

"What happened?" asked George.

Ben said, "We had been married for three years. We liked each other well enough. But we argued all the time. We kept fighting about things."

"I wouldn't worry about it," said George. "She probably won't find you now." George laughed. "And even if she does, she won't get much. You don't have any money."

"Money?" said Ben. "*She's* the one who has money. I just learned that she's rich! This morning I met a shipmate I hadn't seen for years. He told me he ran into my wife a month ago. It seems that she worked for a **wealthy** lady for fifteen years. Then the lady died and left all her money to my wife."

Ben shook his head. "She's rich! I've been working at sea day and night. And for the last twenty years, she's been living in **comfort**."

"Perhaps she'll take you back," said George.

"Take me back?" repeated Ben. "Of course she'll take me back. She'll have to! We're still married." He paused. "At least, I think we still are."

"Well," said George. "Thirty-five years is a long time."

He thought for a moment. Then he said, "Take my **advice.** Don't tell her exactly what happened. Say you were lost at sea. Say that when you came back **afterward,** you couldn't find her."

"That sounds like a good idea," said Ben.

"If you like, I'll come along with you," said George. "I don't have anything to do. If you want, I'll tell her I was lost at sea with you. I'll do anything to help a friend."

"You can come along," said Ben. "She lives not far from here. We could take a bus. Do you have any money?"

George shook his head. "I'm afraid not," he said.

"Well, I guess we can walk," said Ben.

"Just think about it," said George, as they went on their way. "Soon you'll have plenty of money in your pockets." Ben's face brightened. George said, "You'll have enough money to help a friend—a friend like me if I needed some money."

Ten minutes later they were at the gate of a large house. Both men walked slowly up the path. Then George knocked on the door.

A maid answered his knock. She looked closely at the two men. "We don't want to buy anything today," she said. Then she slammed the door in their faces.

"I'll have her fired right away," Ben muttered to himself.

He knocked again and again until the maid opened the door.

"I want to see the lady of the house," Ben said loudly.

"What for?" demanded the maid.

Ben put his foot in the door. "Tell her," he said, "that there are two gentlemen here with news about her husband."

"They were lost with him," said George.

"On a desert island," said Ben.

"In the middle of the ocean," added George.

The two men came in. They sat down in the comfortable chairs. They looked with wide eyes at the beautiful furniture in the room.

"Listen," said George. "Don't tell her who you are right away. You don't want her to faint or anything like that. Let her find out very slowly."

Ben seemed a little nervous. "Perhaps you better speak first," he told George. "She might recognize my voice. Start with a few good words about me. Tell her I always wondered about what had happened to her."

"Quiet!" said George. "Here she comes now."

The door opened. A tall lady with white hair marched into the room. She stood looking at them.

She had changed a great deal in thirty-five years. Ben stared at her. She was wearing a fine black silk dress, a gold watch, and a large diamond pin.

"Good—good afternoon, ma'am," said George very softly.

The lady greeted them. She sat down and watched them very calmly.

"We—we called to see you about a dear old friend," said George. "One of the best. The *best*!"

"Yes?" said the lady.

"He has been missing," said George, "for thirty-five years. Thirty-five years ago—very much against his will—he left his young and beautiful wife to go to sea. His ship was wrecked, and he was lost on a desert island."

"Yes?" said the lady.

"I was lost," said George. "*Both* of us were lost with him. We were on that island for longer than I like to think about. But we were rescued at last. Ever since then he has been hunting high and low for his wife."

"It's all very interesting," said the lady. "But what has that got to do with me?"

"You haven't heard his name yet," said George. "What would you say if I said it was—Ben Davis?"

"I would say it wasn't true," said the lady.

"Not true?" said George. There was pain in his voice.

"About the desert island, I mean," the lady said calmly. "The story I heard was that he went off and left his young wife to do the best she could for herself. I suppose he has heard that she now has a great deal of money."

"*Money*?" said George. He hoped his voice showed surprise. "Did you say *money*?"

"Money!" said the lady. "And I suppose he sent you to try to get some of it."

She was looking straight at Ben as she spoke.

"You didn't know him, or you wouldn't talk that way," said George. "You probably wouldn't recognize him if you saw him now, I suppose."

"I probably wouldn't know him," said the lady.

"Perhaps you would recognize his voice," said Ben Davis at last, breaking his silence.

The lady shook her head. "I understand it wasn't always a pleasant voice. It was always finding fault."

"There might have been faults on *both* sides," said Mr. Davis. "*You* weren't all that you should have been, you know."

"*Me?*" said the lady. "*Me?*"

"Yes, *you*," said Ben, getting up from the chair. "Don't you know me, Mary? Why I recognized you the moment you came into the room."

He moved toward her, but she got up and moved back.

"Stay away from me!" she said, firmly. "Why I've never seen you before in my life!"

"It's Ben Davis, ma'am. It's really him," said George.

"And I've come back!" said Ben Davis. "You're not my husband," she said. "You've made a mistake. You better go! If you don't go at once, I'll send for the police!"

"The police!" said Ben.

"The police!" said the lady. "And I'll call my husband. He won't stand for any of your nonsense. I can tell you that!"

"Your husband!" exclaimed Ben.

"You say you recognize me as your wife," said the lady.

"Certainly," said Ben.

"That's strange," said the lady. "Very strange, indeed. Are you sure? Look again."

Ben looked closely. Then he said, "Yes, of course. I'm certain!"

"That is very strange," said the lady. "But I suppose we do look a little alike. You see, Mrs. Davis is away on vacation right now. I'm just looking after her house. My name happens to be Smith."

Ben stood there amazed. His mouth was wide open.

There was silence for a moment. Then George spoke.

"We all make mistakes," said George. "And

Ben's eyes aren't what they used to be. You see, while we were on that desert island—"

"When—when will she be back?" asked Ben.

The lady looked puzzled. "But I thought you were certain that *I* was your wife," she said.

"My mistake," said Ben. "When will she be back?"

Mrs. Smith shook her head. "I can't say," she answered. "When she's on vacation, I never know exactly when she'll return. Shall I tell her you called?"

"Yes," said Ben. "I'll come back in a week and see if she's here."

"She might be away for months," said the lady. She opened the door. "Good afternoon—gentlemen."

Mr. Davis returned a week later—alone. He stopped at the gate and looked at the FOR SALE sign. He walked up the path. He knocked on the door and was let into the house. A moment later, he stood in front of Mrs. Smith.

"Is she back yet?" he asked.

The lady shook her head.

"Why is there a FOR SALE sign?" demanded Mr. Davis.

"She is thinking of selling the house," said Mrs. Smith. "I let her know that you had been here—and that is the result. She won't come back. You won't see her again."

"Where is she?" asked Mr. Davis.

Mrs. Smith shook her head again. "There's no use telling you," she said. "The money she has is hers. The law won't let you touch a penny of it against her will. Why did you leave her?"

"Why?" said Mr. Davis. "We had some terrible fights."

"I suppose she had a very bad temper in those days," said the lady.

"Yes," said Mr. Davis. "We both had bad tempers. I had a bad temper too."

Mr. Davis stood there for some time. He was deep in thought. "I don't know what it is," he said at last. "But there is something about you that reminds me of her. I was expecting to see her. I guess that's it."

"Well, I won't keep you," said Mrs. Smith. "There is no need for you to come back. I don't want to hurt your feelings. But you don't look as though you are doing too well. Your coat is torn. Your pants are ripped. And your shoes are falling apart. I don't know what people must think!"

"I—I only came to look for my wife," Mr. Davis said, weakly. "I won't come back again."

"And if she should happen to ask what you are doing, what shall I say?"

"Just tell her what you said about my clothes," Mr. Davis answered. "She will understand. She has known what it is to be poor herself. She had a bad temper. But she had a good heart. A *very* good heart. She would never make fun of a man who was poor. Good afternoon, ma'am."

"Good afternoon, *Ben*," said the woman in a voice that had changed.

Ben quickly turned around and stood staring at her.

There was a long silence.

"I've decided to take you back," his wife finally said.

"Why, Mary," said Ben. "What—what made you change your mind?"

Mrs. Davis smiled and said, "Only two people in the world knew I had a good heart. One of them died and left me her fortune. Now I've decided to share it with the other."

And though Ben was a tough old sailor, there were tears in the corners of his eyes.

LOOKING FOR FACTS IN THE STORY. How well can you find facts in a story? Put an *x* in the box next to the right answer.

1. Ben was surprised to learn that
   - ❑ a. his wife had become rich.
   - ❑ b. George was getting married.
   - ❑ c. his ship had left for sea.

2. George told the lady that he and Ben
   - ❑ a. had just arrived in town.
   - ❑ b. thought the house was beautiful.
   - ❑ c. had been lost on a desert island.

3. The lady said that Mrs. Davis
   - ❑ a. was away on vacation.
   - ❑ b. was feeling ill.
   - ❑ c. would be back in a day.

4. Ben said that his wife
   - ❑ a. never got angry.
   - ❑ b. had a very good heart.
   - ❑ c. would make fun of a man who was poor.

EXAMINING VOCABULARY WORDS. Here are four vocabulary questions. Put an *x* in the box next to the right answer. The vocabulary words are printed in **boldface** in the story. You may look back at the words before you answer the questions.

1. A wealthy lady left her money to Mary. The word *wealthy* means
   - ❑ a. healthy.
   - ❑ b. rich.
   - ❑ c. old.

2. She had money and lived in comfort. The word *comfort* means
   - ❑ a. with many problems.
   - ❑ b. in different places.
   - ❑ c. in an easy, pleasant way.

3. George said, "Take my advice and say you were lost at sea." The word *advice* means
   - ❑ a. ideas about what should be done.
   - ❑ b. good wishes.
   - ❑ c. very bad luck.

4. Years afterward, he looked for her. The word *afterward* means
   - ❑ a. later.
   - ❑ b. sorry.
   - ❑ c. poor.

	x 5 =	
NUMBER CORRECT		**YOUR SCORE**

	x 5 =	
NUMBER CORRECT		**YOUR SCORE**

131

A DDING WORDS TO A PARAGRAPH.

Complete the paragraph below. Fill in each blank with one of the words in the box. Each word appears in the story. There are five words and four blanks, so one word in the box will not be used.

Ferdinand Magellan was one of

the greatest _____
1

who ever lived. In 1519 the King of

Spain gave Magellan five

_____. One of
2

these became the first to travel

around the _____ .
3

Although Magellan died before the

_____ journey was
4

completed, he is remembered for

leading the voyage.

world	sailors	ocean
	expecting	ships

	x **5** =	
NUMBER CORRECT		**YOUR SCORE**

R EADING BETWEEN THE LINES.

These questions will help you think critically. You will have to think about what happened in the story, and then figure out the answers. Put an *x* in the box next to the right answer.

1. Which sentence is true?
   - ❑ a. Mrs. Davis was away.
   - ❑ b. Mrs. Davis pretended that she was Mrs. Smith.
   - ❑ c. Mrs. Davis sold the house.

2. When the lady said Mrs. Davis had money, George
   - ❑ a. said he knew about that.
   - ❑ b. borrowed ten dollars.
   - ❑ c. tried to act surprised.

3. We may infer (figure out) that the lady
   - ❑ a. was trying to get rid of Ben and George.
   - ❑ b. believed George's story.
   - ❑ c. really had another husband.

4. Ben said Mrs. Smith reminded him of his wife. Probably this was because
   - ❑ a. "Mrs. Smith" *was* his wife.
   - ❑ b. The women were sisters.
   - ❑ c. Ben didn't see very well.

	x **5** =	
NUMBER CORRECT		**YOUR SCORE**

N OTING STORY ELEMENTS.

Some story elements are **plot, character, setting,** and **mood.** Put an *x* in the box next to the right answer.

1. What happened last in the *plot*?
   - ❑ a. Ben said his wife was rich.
   - ❑ b. The lady said that Ben's shoes were falling apart.
   - ❑ c. Ben saw a FOR SALE sign.

2. Which sentence *characterizes* Mrs. Davis?
   - ❑ a. She was short and shy.
   - ❑ b. She was tall and very well dressed.
   - ❑ c. She believed everything that people told her.

3. What is the *setting* of the story?
   - ❑ a. a ship
   - ❑ b. a large house
   - ❑ c. a bench in the street

4. Which sentence tells the *theme*?
   - ❑ a. A sailor is lost at sea.
   - ❑ b. A woman says she will call the police.
   - ❑ c. A man tries to win back his wife by telling lies, but the story ends happily.

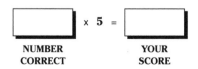

	x **5** =	
NUMBER CORRECT		**YOUR SCORE**

THINKING MORE ABOUT THE STORY. Your teacher might want you to write your answers.

◆ George and Ben tried to trick Mrs. Davis, but she tricked them instead. Explain how that happened.

◆ "For Better or Worse" is both funny and serious. Give examples from the story to show this is true.

◆ Why did Mary finally decide to take Ben back? Do you believe that they will be happy together now? Why?

Use the boxes below to total your scores for the exercises. Then write your score on pages 136 and 137.

☐ +	**L** OOKING FOR FACTS IN THE STORY
☐ +	**E** XAMINING VOCABULARY WORDS
☐ +	**A** DDING WORDS TO A PARAGRAPH
☐ +	**R** EADING BETWEEN THE LINES
☐ ▼	**N** OTING STORY ELEMENTS
☐	**SCORE TOTAL:** Story 12

Acknowledgments

Acknowledgment is gratefully made to the following publishers, authors, and agents for permission to reprint these works. Adaptations and/or abridgments are by Burton Goodman.

"Playmate" by Leslie A. Croutch. Reprinted by permission of Forrest J. Ackerman, 2495 Glendower Ave., Hollywood, CA 90027-1110.

"How Now Purple Cow" by Bill Pronzini. Reprinted by permission of Larry Sternig and Jack Byrne Literary Agency.

"Trapped" by Carmen Hansen from *Literary Cavalcade*, 1960. Copyright © 1960 by Scholastic Inc. Reprinted by permission of the publisher.

"The Jade Goddess" by Lin Yutang from *Famous Chinese Short Stories* by Lin Yutang. Copyright © 1948, 1951, 1952 by (John Day Co.) Harper & Row Publishers, Inc. Reprinted by permission of Taiyi Lin Lai and Hsiang Ju Lin for the Estate of Lin Yutang.

"The Mirror" from *Tales for the Midnight Hour* by J. B. Stamper. Copyright © 1992 by J. B. Stamper. Reprinted by permission of Scholastic Inc.

"Ortega's Fortune" by Manuela Williams Crosno, adapted by Burton Goodman. Copyright © 1987 by Manuela Williams Crosno. Used by permission of Burton Goodman, agent for Mrs. Crosno.

"Watch Out!" by Bruce Coville. Copyright © 1987 by Bruce Coville. First appeared in slightly different form in *Spaceships & Spells*, edited by Jane Yolen, Martin H. Greenberg, and Charles Waugh. (Harper & Row, 1987.)

Progress Chart

1. Write in your score for each exercise.
2. Write in your Score Total.

	L	E	A	R	N	TOTAL SCORE
Story 1						
Story 2						
Story 3						
Story 4						
Story 5						
Story 6						
Story 7						
Story 8						
Story 9						
Story 10						
Story 11						
Story 12						

Progress Graph

1. Write your Score Total in the box under the number for each story.
2. Put an *x* along the line above each box to show your Score Total for that story.
3. Make a graph of your progress by drawing a line to connect the *x*'s.

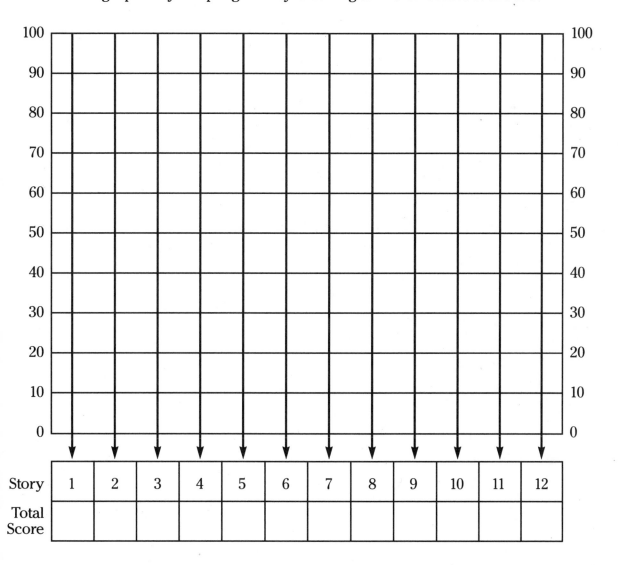